the ETC program

Language and Culture in Depth

A Competency-Based Reading/Writing Book

Elaine Kirn
West Los Angeles College

Joanna Vellone McKenzie
California State University, Northridge
Reseda Community Adult School

RANDOM HOUSE New York

First Edition

9 8 7 6 5 4 3 2

Library of Congress Cataloging-in-Publication Data

Kirn, Elaine.
    The *ETC* program. Language and culture in depth ; a
competency-based reading writing book

    Level 5.
    1. English language—Textbooks for foreign speakers.
2. Reading   (Adult education)   I. McKenzie, Joanna
Vellone.   II. Title.
PE1128.K4828   1989   428.6'4   88-29819
ISBN 0-394-35357-9 (Student Edition)
ISBN 0-394-38068-1 (Teacher's Edition)

Manufactured in the United States of America

Series design and production: Etcetera Graphics
                        Canoga Park, California

Cover design: Juan Vargas, Vargas/Williams Design

Illustrations: Etcetera Graphics

Artist: Terry Wilson

Typesetting: Etcetera Graphics

Contents

CHAPTER 8   Having Fun   **99**

Competencies/Skills: Recognizing the order of steps in instructions ● Recognizing and understanding idioms (using the dictionary) ● Arranging information to attract attention ● Arranging steps in instructions ● Using connecting words of time order

CHAPTER 9   The Media   **111**

Competencies/Skills: Recognizing the organization of points ● Recognizing the meaning of word parts (prefixes, stems, and suffixes) ● Writing general statements for essays ● Writing topic sentences for paragraphs ● Outlining ● Using connecting words (*furthermore, in addition, however,* etc.) and punctuation (semicolons)

CHAPTER 10   A Lifetime of Learning   **124**

Competencies/Skills: Distinguishing attempts to persuade from facts ● Distinguishing objective from subjective language ● Using adjective, noun, and adverb clauses

Preface

Language is me.
Language is you.
Language is people.
Language is what people do.
Language is loving and hurting.
Language is clothes, faces, gestures, responses.
Language is imagining, designing, creating, destroying.
Language is control and persuasion.
Language is communication.
Language is laughter.
Language is growth.
Language is me.
The limits of my language are the limits of my world.

And you can't package *that* up in a book, can you?

—New Zealand Curriculum Development

No, you can't package language in a book or even a whole program of books, but you have to start somewhere.

About the *ETC* Program

ETC is a six-level ESL (English as a second language) program for adults who are learning English to improve their lives and work skills. The material of each level is divided into two or three books, carefully coordinated, chapter by chapter, in theme, competency goals, grammar, and vocabulary. For a visual representation of the scope and sequence of the program, see the back cover of any volume.

ETC has been designed for maximum efficiency and flexibility. To choose the materials most suitable for your particular teaching situation, decide on the appropriate level by assessing the ability and needs of the students you expect to be teaching. The competency descriptions included in each instructor's manual ("About This Level") will aid you in your assessment.

About This Book

ETC Language and Culture in Depth: A Competency-Based Reading/Writing Book offers two kinds of reading material: first, there are background readings in story form about practical situations, such as getting a loan, applying for a promotion, opening a business, visiting a travel agency, and so on; the comprehension exercises that follow focus on getting the main ideas, recognizing time order, relevant points, reasons, steps in a process, and organization; and other comprehension skills related to "rhetorical forms." Second, there are scanning exercises based on unsimplified realia, such as calendars of events, school information, credit statements, legal agreements, and the like.

The vocabulary sections begin with skills taught at lower levels, such as recognizing synonyms and parts of speech and guessing meaning from context, and gradually progress to more sophisticated topics of interest to upper-level students—recognizing the connotations of words, "shades of meaning," the precise meaning of specialized language, idioms, and the like.

The writing sections, closely correlated with the "rhetorical forms" (narration, argument, comparison, etc.) presented in the reading, give students the opportunity to combine their ideas and language skills in a variety of forms; these concentrate on businesses and personal letters but also include personal journals, autobiographies, simple "legal" agreements, and flyers. Students learn to organize their thoughts in a first draft and to follow suggested steps to edit their own grammar and to improve their writing style.

Organization

Like most other books in the *ETC* program, *ETC Language and Culture in Depth: A Competency-Based Reading/Writing Book* consists of an introduction and ten chapters, each divided into four parts with specific purposes.

- *Part One: Reading for Meaning* offers an illustrated "warm-up" activity for the purpose of previewing the reading, a background reading that often includes a "writing model" for later reference, and comprehension and discussion activities.

- *Part Two: Vocabulary Building* presents vocabulary exercises in various forms, including dictionary activities.

- *Part Three: Scanning for Information* consists of various kinds of realia with questions along with suggestions for "beyond the text" reading activities.

- *Part Four: Expressing Yourself in Writing* includes ideas to help students organize their thoughts, grammar correction exercises, and steps to follow in the process of learning to compose in English.

Symbols

The following symbol appears throughout the text:

✱ a challenging beyond-the-text activity designed for more advanced students

Available Ancillaries

The instructor's manual for this text includes:

- a general introduction to the *ETC* program, this level, and this book

- general suggestions for teaching techniques to use in presenting the various kinds of activities

- an answer key for all text exercises with definite answers

- progress tests, one to accompany each chapter of the text, which can be duplicated and distributed to all students

- an answer key to all progress tests

Acknowledgments

To Etcetera, ETC, ETC, because we finally did it.

Appreciation beyond frustration goes to the many class testers and reviewers, reviewers, reviewers—whose opinions lie at the core of the *ETC* program. Thanks to the following reviewers, whose comments both favorable and critical, were of great value in the development of *ETC Language and Culture in Depth*:

Roberta Alexander, Saeed M. Ali, Carol Brots, Patricia Costello, Lorelei A. De Pauw, Marjorie S. Fuchs, Mary M. Hurst, Darcy Jack, C.A. Johnston, Gail Kellersberger, Dona Kelley, Renee Klosz, Kara Rosenberg, Saul Sanchez, Collins W. Selby, Cheryl L. Sexton, Jackie Stembridge, and Kent Sutherland.

The authors wish to thank the staff at Random House:
- Eirik Borve and Karen Judd—for keeping promises,
- Lesley Walsh—for being as efficient as ever,
- Marian Hartsough—for communicating where need be, and
- Cynthia Ward, Marianne Taflinger, and the sales staff—for what is yet to come.

Heartfelt thanks to the staff and supporters of Etcetera Graphics, Canoga Park, California:
- Joy Gilliam—for careful copyediting,
- Terry Wilson—for his inspired artwork and patience,
- Cindra Tardif—for expert typesetting, and
- Christopher Young—for alert and patient production,

and gratitude, appreciation, and love to
- Anthony Thorne-Booth—for his management, expertise, and hard work,
- Karol Roff—for helping, helping, helping,
- Sally Kostal—for jumping in to rescue us and to keep us calm,
- Chuck Alessio—for everything and more.

To Andi Kirn and Rod McKenzie—for putting up with it all.

E.K. and J.M.

About Reading and Writing

READING SKILLS: Previewing
Getting the main ideas
Building vocabulary
Scanning for information

WRITING SKILLS: Understanding the writing process

Fluent Reading

Reading is a basic tool in adult life. Every day most people need to read signs, labels, instructions, forms, schedules, rules and regulations, and so forth. At work there may also be necessary paperwork: letters, reports, agreements, announcements, and other forms of written communication. In addition, many people get the current news not only from T.V. and radio but also from daily or weekly newspapers. Some also read magazines, while others enjoy novels or other fiction. And of course, students are required to read textbooks and assignment instructions.

Good readers read a lot and enjoy the process, but adults who have not acquired the skills necessary for fluency, especially in a language other than their native one, may not like to read. Yet most of these readers can improve their skills if they use a few simple techniques.

Previewing

Fluent readers use their minds more than their eyes. They not only see the words and sentences, but they also think as they read. "Previewing" is a prereading activity that helps them to "anticipate" (to form predictions about what they are going to read). To preview, look at titles, subtitles, pictures, words in large or bold print, or anything else that catches your eye. From this information, you can make guesses about the contents of an article, a chapter, or a book.

A. **To preview this textbook and this introductory chapter, find the answers to these questions as quickly as possible and write them on the lines.**

1. What is the title of the book? *ETC Language and Culture in Depth*

   What is the subtitle? _____

   From the title and subtitle, what do you think the book is about? _____

   _____

   _____

2. Who are the authors of this book? _____

   _____ Who is the publisher? _____ In what

   year was the book last published? _____ Where did you get the information for

   Item 2? _____

3. Is this book part of a larger program? _____ If so, how many books are there in the

   program? _____ How do you know this information? _____

   _____

4. How many chapters are there in this book? _____ Which chapter is about "Getting Help"? _____ About "The Media"? _____ What is Chapter 1 about? _____ _____ Chapter 6? _____ Which chapters interest you the most? _____ _____ _____ Why? _____ _____What is the name of the part of the book that gives you the information for Item 4? _____

5. What are two of the reading skills or techniques that this introduction discusses? _____ _____ _____ Where did you get the information for the last question? _____

Getting the Main Ideas

Whenever you read anything for more than enjoyment, you may want to skim it (read it quickly for general meaning) before you look at it more carefully. Even if you don't understand every word or sentence, you should try to understand the important ideas, especially on the first reading. You might want to reread something several times for extra practice, but it's not usually necessary to understand or remember all the details, especially if they are not important to the purpose of your reading.

B. **Do you remember the main ideas in this introduction so far? For each sentence, cross out the letter of the words that would *not* be correct in the sentence.**

1. Some common kinds of reading material are ____.
   a. signs, ads, instructions, and forms
   ~~b.~~ T.V. and radio
   c. newspapers, magazines, and textbooks

2. Adults who ____ may not enjoy the reading process.
   a. read many novels and other fiction
   b. have not acquired the skills necessary for fluency
   c. don't know the techniques to use to improve their skills

3. Fluent readers use ____.
   a. their minds more than their eyes
   b. their eyes to see and understand every word
   c. the technique of "previewing" to form predictions

4. To preview, a reader looks quickly at ____.
   a. titles and pictures
   b. words in large or bold print
   c. the sentences that don't catch the eye right away

5. Whenever you read anything, you should ____.
   a. skim or read quickly to get the general meaning
   b. read every sentence twice before you start the next sentence
   c. not try to understand or remember every unimportant detail

---

Building Vocabulary

There are many ways to learn new vocabulary. For example, you can learn synonyms (words with similar meanings) for words you already know and expressions with those words. To guess the approximate meaning of new vocabulary, you should pay attention to the part of speech (noun, verb, adjective, adverb, etc.), the meanings of the word parts (prefix, stem, and suffix), and the context clues (the other words in the same sentence or paragraph). Although you shouldn't rely on a dictionary when you are reading quickly for main ideas, you may want to use one later to look up new words. You can find out several things: the definition of the word, the shades of meaning (the slightly different uses of synonyms), examples of the word in context, and so on.

C. Follow these instructions to learn more about the vocabulary in the sections you just read.

On the line, write the part of speech (*n* = noun, *v* = verb, *adj* = adjective, *adv* = adverb) for each of these words.

1. *n* paperwork

2. *adj* necessary

3. _____ current

4. _____ skim

5. _____ quickly

6. _____ reread

7. _____ fluent

8. _____ fluency

9. _____ carefully

In the sections on "Fluent Reading" and "Previewing," find words that are related to these words but are different parts of speech. Write them on the lines.

10. *v*: announce / *n*: _____

11. *v*: agree / *n*: _____

12: *n*: day / *adj*: _____

13: *n*: enjoyment / *v*: _____

14. *adj*: special / *adv*: _____

15. *v*: read / *n*: _____

16. *adj*: active / *n*: _____

17. *v*: contain / *n*: _____

Do the words or expressions in each of the following pairs have similar meanings? Write *yes* or *no* on the lines.

18. *yes* novels / fiction

19. _____ native / language

20. _____ be required to / have to

21. _____ preview / anticipate

22. _____ chapter / subtitle

23. _____ discuss / talk about

24. _____ general / specific

25. _____ get / acquire

Scanning for Information

Most adults need to acquire a large amount of information from practical reading material, but they do not have the time or the interest to read every word. Most information gathering is scanning (finding information as quickly as possible for a specific purpose). To scan, you should move your eyes quickly to pick out appropriate clues.

D. Scan the chart to find out information about the book. Fill in the blanks in the sentences that follow.

	Organization of Skills			
	PART ONE Reading Skills	**PART TWO** Vocabulary	**PART THREE** Scanning	**PART FOUR** Writing Skills
Chapter 1	Previewing Getting the main ideas Understanding details	Synonyms Descriptive words Parts of speech	Calendars of events	Verb tenses Basic capitalization and punctuation Paragraph form
Chapter 2	Recognizing time order		School information	Autobiographies Time expressions Combining sentences
Chapter 3	Business letters	Business language Nouns used as adjectives	Credit statements	Phrases that introduce additional information
Chapter 4	Letters of application	"Impressive" vocabulary Related words	Employment ads	Writing concisely Resumes
Chapter 5	Legal agreements	Legal vocabulary	Legal agreements	Written agreements

1. This chart shows the skills introduced in ____ chapters of ____ parts each.

2. You will practice the skill of "recognizing time order" in Chapter ____. You will learn "business language" in Chapter ____ and "basic capitalization and punctuation" in Chapter ____.

3. In general, Part Two teaches _____, and Part Three teaches _____.

4. You'll learn to write an autobiography in Part _____ of Chapter ____. In Part Four of Chapter 5, you'll learn to write _____.

E. Ask one another questions about the information in the chart in Exercise D. Find the answers as fast as you can.

The Writing Process

Most adults write for practical purposes (memos, agreements, business letters, etc.), to communicate with others (postcards, personal letters, etc.), and to organize their ideas and thoughts or improve their language skills (journals, essays, etc.).The writing process can consist of several steps: gathering ideas, writing thoughts as they come to mind, organizing those thoughts into a first draft, rereading and correcting what you wrote, and making a final copy with your corrections and improvements.

F. You can follow these steps to get to know some of your classmates.

1. If you have a chance to tell your classmates about yourself, what will you say? On a piece of paper, write about yourself for five minutes. Don't worry about grammar and other writing rules at first. Just put down your ideas as they come to mind. **Example:**

    I arrived in this country a short time ago. In my country, I have many relatives and friends. I miss them very much. I miss my house, my school, and the people I worked with at my job. Sometimes when I'm eating a hamburger, I think about the food in my country, and I get even more homesick. I'm living with my family in a large apartment complex on a busy street. There are many people there, but I'm too shy to meet them. Anyway, they don't seem friendly except to the people they already know.

2. Reread your writing to find the most important idea. On the other side of your paper, write a phrase for that idea (**Example:** meeting people in a new place).

3. In your writing, underline the sentences that are part of that one idea. List them in logical order and add other related thoughts and ideas that come to mind. **Examples:**

    - arrived a short time ago
    - miss my relatives and friends
    - miss people at my job
    - many people in our building
    - too shy to meet them
    - don't seem friendly
    - no feeling of community

4. Write the ideas in your list in paragraph form. Make corrections if you have time. **Example:**

    I arrived in this country a short time ago. In my country, I have many relatives and friends—in the neighborhood, at school, and at work, and I miss them very much. Now I'm living with my family in a large apartment complex where there are many people, but I'm too shy to meet the neighbors. Maybe it's because I'm not used to the customs in this new culture, but my neighbors don't seem friendly except to the people they already know. There doesn't seem to be the same feeling of community that exists in my hometown.

5. Pass your paper to the classmate on your right. Read the paper you receive. Write down notes or try to remember the important information. Then pass that paper to the classmate on your right, read the information on the next paper you receive, and so on. Repeat this process until your teacher tells you to stop.

6. Your instructor will collect the papers and tell you facts from some of them. Try to identify the writers.

Meeting People

READING AND WRITING FOCUS:	Personal journals
NEW READING AND VOCABULARY SKILLS:	Previewing* Getting the main ideas* Understanding important details Recognizing synonyms, descriptive words, and parts of speech Scanning calendars of events
WRITING SKILLS:	Choosing verb tenses Using basic capitalization and punctuation Using paragraph form
GRAMMAR FOCUS:	Verb tenses (present and past—simple and continuous, future)

*reinforced in all following chapters

PART ONE / READING FOR MEANING

● Finding New Friends

Previewing the Reading

A.   Prepare to read by making up a story about the pictures. Answer these questions.

1.   Who are the people? What are they doing? Why?
2.   How are they probably feeling?

B. Read the following selection quickly for important ideas.

Hong Trinh Dang has been in the United States for about a month. Since he arrived, he has been keeping a journal of his experiences and thoughts. Here are some of his journal entries.

Monday, July 11, 19XX

I've just arrived in Los Angeles, California, and I'm eager to make some new friends! I'm living with my brother Long, his wife, and their three sons in their small apartment. It's in a large building. There are many other people living there, but they never look or smile at me. I'm afraid to speak to them because they seem unfriendly.

Thursday, July 21

Yesterday I went to the River Park Church with my brother and his family, and Long introduced me to some of his acquaintances. They were friendly to me, even though they don't know Long very well. But they're older than I am, and we didn't seem to have much in common. I'd like to meet some people my own age.

Thursday, August 11

I have a tedious job working on the assembly line of the small computer firm where my brother works. There are many people working there at my company, but it's difficult for me to talk with them. At breaks most of my coworkers chatter away but only to each other. They don't seem to want new people like me to break into their group.

In Vietnam I had many friends. How I miss them now! My eyes water and I get a lump in my throat when I recall our happy times together. Once when my best friend Thao was working for the government, he invited another friend and me to take a ride with him in the limousine of an official. That luxurious car had a built-in bar and a magnificient stereo system with a terrific tape deck. I'll never forget how comfortable I was feeling as we sped along the road like wealthy people. I leaned back against the plush velvet upholstery, sipped a cool drink, and tapped my feet to the rhythm of my favorite music.

How lonely those happy memories make me feel now! I'm going to try to make some new friends here, but I don't know how to meet people.

Friday, August 26

Today a guy from my country joined our assembly line. It was a relief to be able to speak Vietnamese for a change. Michael uses an American name and speaks English almost fluently. He invited me to go to a baseball game with him and some of his buddies. I'm going to have to make more of an effort to meet people who share my interests. Perhaps the ball game will be a good beginning.

Saturday, September 3

I went to the ball game at Stanley Stadium last night and met two of Michael's buddies there. It's usually difficult for me to have conversations in English, but I didn't have any trouble talking with them because we have a lot in common. We all like baseball, fishing, and rock music. We're planning to get tickets for a concert.

Sunday, September 11

How different my life in this country seems now that I have some friends! This afternoon my three new pals and I had lunch together. Then some of Michael's acquaintances joined us and we went to Mile High Lake to fish. We all exchanged phone numbers and made plans to meet this weekend at Sierra Park. They also invited me to a party they're having next month. I'm so glad I went to that baseball game!

C. *Getting the Main Ideas*—Circle the letter of the correct words for each blank.

1. When he first arrived in the United States, Hong found it _____ to make new friends.
   a. easy
   b. difficult
   c. unnecessary

2. The happy memories he had of his friends in his country made him feel _____.
   a. lonely
   b. eager
   c. afraid

3. Hong's first friend in the United States is _____.
   a. a woman who changed her name and speaks fluent English
   b. an American baseball player who likes rock music
   c. a man from his country who works in his company

4. Hong didn't have any trouble talking with Michael's friends because _____.
   a. they are from his country
   b. they had concert tickets
   c. he has interests in common with them

5. Now that Hong has some friends in this country, his life seems _____.
   a. different
   b. more tedious
   c. more difficult

D. *Understanding Details*—Write *T* (true) or *F* (false) on each line and correct the false statements.

1. _*F*_ Hong started his journal ~~two months after~~ *as soon as* he arrived in the United States.

2. _____ He's living in a big house with his two brothers.

3. _____ At his brother's church, he met some people his own age, but they weren't very friendly to him.

4. _____ It wasn't easy for Hong to break into the group of workers at his company.

5. _____ One of his happy memories is of a rock concert a year ago.

6. _____ Hong's coworker Michael invited him to a baseball game with some buddies.

7. _____ Hong, Michael, and a group of friends have made some plans for future activities.

E. Now that you have read Hong's journal, look back at the pictures on page 8 and retell his story.

F. *Expressing Your Own Ideas*—Check each of the following statements that you agree with. In small groups, discuss the reasons for your answers. Then summarize your discussion for the class.

1. _____ When you start a new life, it's a good idea to write down your experiences and thoughts in a journal.

2. _____ Loneliness can be a big problem when you move to a new place.

3. _____ You shouldn't think about your life and friends in your old country because happy memories will make you sad.

4. _____ It's easy to make new friends in another country if you have a big family.

5. _____ If you want to meet new people, you have to break into their groups.

6. _____ It's best to make friends with people of your own age who speak the same native language.

PART TWO / VOCABULARY BUILDING

● Synonyms ● Descriptive Words ● Parts of Speech

> To read fluently, you shouldn't rely on your dictionary because looking up words will slow down your reading. Instead, you should try to guess the meaning of new vocabulary from *context*—the other words in the same sentence or paragraph. Sometimes you will find *synonyms* there, words with the same meanings. For example, the two new words in the above sentences are explained by other words. *Context* means "the other words in the same sentence or paragraph." *Synonyms* means "words with the same meanings."

A. Underline the two synonyms in each sentence.

1. I work for a computer <u>firm</u> but I haven't met many of my coworkers in the <u>company</u>.

2. I've never ridden in a more luxurious car than that government limousine.

3. It had a magnificent stereo system and a terrific bar.

4. The rich upholstery made me feel like a wealthy person.

5. My pals and I went with some new buddies to a nearby lake.

> To create a picture in the minds of the readers, most writers include descriptive words.
>
> **Example:**
>
> At breaks most of my coworkers chatter away but only to each other. (*Chatter* means "to talk quickly, often about unimportant things." It is a less common, but more descriptive, word than *talk*.)

B. Replace the underlined words with more descriptive words from this list.

leaned	luxurious	plush	tapped
sipped	water	sped	get a lump in my throat

How wealthy I felt as we ~~drove fast~~ *sped* along the road in that <u>very comfortable</u> car! I
<u>1.</u>   <u>2.</u>

<u>sat back</u> against the <u>soft</u> velvet seat, <u>slowly drank</u> a cold drink, and <u>moved</u> my feet to the
<u>3.</u>   <u>4.</u>   <u>5.</u>   <u>6.</u>

rhythm of the music. When I remember that happy experience, my eyes <u>get wet</u>, and I
<u>7.</u>

<u>feel emotion.</u>
<u>8.</u>

> To understand the important ideas of a reading selection, it is not usually necessary to know the exact meaning of a new word. If you recognize the part of speech (noun, verb, or adjective), you may be able to guess its general meaning from the context.
>
> **Example:**
>
> He has been writing a journal. (*Journal* is a noun. The general meaning is "something you can write.")

C. To guess the meaning of each underlined word or expression, first decide if it is a noun, verb, or adjective. (Write *n*, *v*, or *adj* on the line.) Then circle the letter of the correct general meaning for that part of speech.

1. I work on the assembly line of a computer firm.
   n   **a.** an area in a company   **b.** put parts together

2. It's a tedious job with long hours.
   _____   **a.** a feeling of boredom   **b.** tiring

3. It was a relief to speak my native language for a change.
   _____   **a.** a good feeling   **b.** relax

4. I feel lonely when I recall our happy times together.
   _____   **a.** memories   **b.** remember

5. I'm going to make more of an effort to meet people.
   _____   **a.** an attempt   **b.** push harder

6. At the ball game, I met some guys who share my interests.
   _____   **a.** a part of something   **b.** have in common

*D. To learn vocabulary, list ten new words from the reading selection "Finding New Friends" or something else you are reading. For each word, look for a synonym in the context. Decide if it is a noun, verb, or adjective. If it is a descriptive word, try to replace it with a more common word. Then write the general meaning. To check your guesses, you can look up the words in your dictionary.

PART THREE / SCANNING FOR INFORMATION

● Calendars of Events

> When you have free time, you can check the calendar of events in a local newspaper for places to go and things to do. If you go to one of these events or participate in one of these activities, you may or may not meet friendly people who share your interests. But you will probably enjoy yourself in any case.

A. Skim these announcements and circle the letters of the events or activities that interest you. Tell the class your choices and explain your reasons.

CALENDAR

Art and Culture

A   Sunday
"**Summer Concerts in the Park**" held at Warner Center, 5800 Topanga Canyon Blvd. in Woodland Hills, will feature The Musical Knights, conducted by Horace Heidt. Music will begin at 5:30 p.m. Information: 704-1358.

Classes

B   Monday
A Basic Wilderness Skills class will be offered during a series of classes to held on Monday evenings. A weekend backpack trip will take place the weekend after the last session. Preregistration is required and there is a $95 fee for the class. For information contact the Wilderness Institute at: 887-7831.

C   Ongoing
The Los Angeles Police Department is co-sponsoring free one-evening self-defense workshops for groups such as churches, clubs, schools/colleges and apartment complexes, at group-obtained facilities. Information: 710-1660.

Pets

D   "**How to Live with Your Dog,**" a 10-week dog-obedience session for dogs 4 months and older, is offered by the county Parks and Recreation Department. Registration and information: (805) 251-2541 or (805) 259-1750.

Senior Citizens

E   **Tuesday Seniors Dance Club** meets at 10:00 a.m. Tuesdays at Valley Beth Isreal, 13060 Roscoe Blvd. The program includes dances such as the cha-cha, tango, rhumba, waltz, fox trot, swing and mambo. Information: 781-7690.

Parks

F   **Balboa Park in Encino** offers a mile-long skate path and a 6-mile bike path for cyclists and skaters. The park is open year-round. For information: call 887-7831.

Children

G   **The Boys and Girls Club** of the San Fernando Valley is open to young people 7 to 17 from 3 to 8 p.m. Tuesdays through Fridays and from 10 a.m. to 3 p.m. Saturdays. The new facility is at 11251 Glenoaks Blvd., Pacoima. Information: 896-5261.

H   **Woodland Hills Parents Co-op** Nursery School offers morning classes Mondays, Wednesdays and Fridays for 4-year olds, and Tuesdays and Thursdays for 3-year olds. Information: 884-7451.

Volunteers

I   **The Los Angeles chapter** of Mothers Against Drunk Driving needs volunteers to answer telephone inquiries from the public and perform general clerical tasks. All volunteers will be trained. Information: 705-MADD (6233), 9 a.m. and 5 p.m. Mondays through Fridays.

J   **The San Fernando Valley** Child Guidance Clinic needs volunteers to serve in the following capacities: tutoring Spanish and English, play-group therapy assistants, receptionists and clerical workers. Information: Vicki Snider at 993-9311.

B. To follow these instructions, scan the announcements in Exercise A for information.

1. Many events and activities are directed toward specific groups. On each line, write the letter of an announcement that might interest these people.

    _G_ _H_ teenagers, children, and parents

    _____ older people

    _____ _____ people who offer to work without pay

    _____ people who keep animals at home

    _____ _____ people who enjoy nature and like to spend time outdoors

2. Schools, clubs, or other organizations often sponsor public events or activities. On each line, write the name of the sponsor.

    Announcement B: _the Wilderness Institute_

    Announcement C: _____

    Announcement E: _____

    Announcement D: _____

3. On each line, write the name of the place for the activity.

    "Summer Concerts in the Park": _Warner Park_

    Seniors Dance Club: _____

    skating and biking: _____

4. Read each situation and answer the question.

    A man was attacked on the street, and now he's afraid. How can he learn to protect himself?

    He can go to a self-defense workshop.

    A woman's son was injured by a drunk driver. She is angry and wants to help prevent such accidents in the future. What can she do?

    _____

    A mother usually stays home with her small son, but she wants him to play with other children. Where can she take him?

    _____

A teacher from Argentina wants to meet
North Americans but he can't get a job. He likes
to help people. What can he do?

_____

A seventy-year-old couple love music and want
some exercise. Where can they enjoy both?

_____

_____ ***C.** **Discuss any vocabulary in the announcements that seems important. Then ask a partner more questions about the events and activities.**

_____ ***D.** **Beyond the text: Bring to class the calendar of events from a local newspaper. List new vocabulary words and find out their meanings. Read one or more announcements aloud to the class and discuss the events. Then go to one of them and describe your experience to the class.**

PART FOUR / EXPRESSING YOURSELF IN WRITING

● Personal Journals

> To record your experiences, express your feelings, and improve your English, you might want to keep a personal journal. You can use a notebook for your journal. Write down the date of each entry first and then write your thoughts for that day or week.

A.   *A First Draft*—To begin a journal entry, you can follow these steps. Don't worry about grammar and other writing rules at first. Just put down your ideas as they come to mind. Leave space between lines so you can make corrections later.

1. Look around the room or outside until you see something that reminds you of a person, place, or event from the past. On a piece of paper, write a word or phrase for it (**Example:** a ride in a limousine).

2. Describe your memory. Keep writing until you fill one page.

3. Reread what you wrote. On the back of your paper, put down one word that describes your feelings about it now (**Example:** homesick). Then write why you feel that way.

4. What future plans come to mind because of your present feelings? Write them in a phrase (**Example:** to call my family). Then write more about those plans.

Verb Tenses

To clarify the time frames of your experiences and thoughts, try to choose the most appropriate verb tenses. You will most often use past forms (simple and continuous) for past events and feelings, present forms (simple and continuous) for present events and feelings, and future forms for future plans.

Examples:

    I'm **looking** (*present continuous*) out the window now, and I **see** (*simple present*) a limousine. Once when my best friend **was working** (*past continuous*) for the government, he **invited** (*simple past*) me to take a ride with him in a car like that. This weekend I'm **going to take** (*future*) a short trip with some new pals. I hope it **will be** (*future*) the start of some long friendships.

B.   For this journal entry, correct the verb tense forms of the underlined words. Then, if necessary, correct the verb tense forms in the journal entry you wrote for Exercise A.

At home I <u>~~was having~~</u> *had* many friends. How I <u>am missing</u> them now! My eyes <u>are</u>
             1.   2.   3.

<u>water</u>, and I <u>got</u> a lump in my throat when I <u>am recalling</u> our happy times together.
            4.   5.

Once when my friend Thao <u>is working</u> for the government, he <u>was invited</u> another pal
                        6.   7.

and me to take a ride with him in a limousine. I <u>not forget</u> how comfortable I <u>was feel</u> as
                                   8.   9.

we <u>speed</u> along the road like wealthy people. How lonely I <u>will feel</u> now! I <u>going have to</u>
   10.   11.   12.

<u>try</u> to make some new friends here.

Basic Capitalization and Punctuation

To express your meaning clearly, you should pay attention to the details of capitalization and punctuation. Here are some basic rules.

1. Capitalize the names of people, languages and nationalities, geographical and specific places, days of the week, and months.

   Examples:

Hong Trinh Dang	Mile High Lake	Wednesday
Vietnamese	the River Park Church	April 26

2. Replace missing letters in a contraction with an apostrophe (').

   Examples:

I've	It's	they're	didn't

3. Use a comma (,) to separate the parts of a date or an address and the items of a series.

   Examples:

Monday, January 5	**my brother, his wife, and**
Los Angeles, California	**their three sons**

4. Begin each sentence with a capital letter and end most statements with a period (.). You can occasionally use an exclamation point (!) to express emotion.

   Examples:

   I have a tedious job. How long my work hours seem!

C. **Capitalize words and add punctuation (' . ! ,) where necessary in this journal entry. Then, if necessary, correct the capitalization and punctuation in your journal entry from Exercise A.**

monday february 16 19XX

how happy I feel when I call old friends yesterday my buddy michael and I

talked for over an hour about some happy memories we recalled a trip to the

ocean park zoo with pedro gonzalez and omar salameh last april we really enjoyed

the indian elephant the african lions and the american eagle then we saw a crowd

of people and went over to them they were surrounding a famous british rock

star the girls were touching him trying to get his autograph and screaming how

young they seemed I can t understand why they wouldn t leave him alone it s fun

to remember good times

Paragraph Form

Most writing is in paragraph form. If you use a separate paragraph for each new topic, your readers will get a clearer picture of your ideas. Indent (leave a space) at the beginning of the first line of a paragraph. Begin all other lines at the left margin and end every line except the last at the right margin. Here is a picture of how a paragraph looks.

     Xxxxxxx X xxxxxxxxxxxx xxxxxx xxxxxx x xxxxxxxxxx. Xxxxx xxxx

xxxxxxxxx xxxxxxx x xxxxxxxxxxxxxxx xxxxx x xxxxxxxxxxxx x

xxxxxxxxxxxxx! Xx xxxxxxxx xx xxxxxxxxx xxxxxxx. Xxxxxxxx xxxx

xxxxxxxx, x xxxxxx xxxxx, x xxxxxxxxxx xxxxx.

D. Rewrite your journal entry from Exercise A in paragraph form, making any necessary corrections and changes. Then exchange papers with a classmate. Your partner will read your entry and ask you questions about it. Discuss your ideas and experiences. Then summarize your discussion for the class.

*E. You may want to begin keeping a journal in a notebook. Every day or every few days, write an entry that describes a past experience, a present feeling, or a future plan. Before you write new entries, you might want to read over some of your past ones.

Getting an Education

READING AND WRITING FOCUS:	School information and forms; autobiographies
NEW READING AND VOCABULARY SKILLS:	Recognizing chronological (time) order
	Recognizing synonyms, descriptive words, and parts of speech
	Scanning school information and forms
WRITING SKILLS:	Putting events in chronological order
	Using time expressions
	Combining sentences (*and*, *but*, *so*)
	Writing questions
GRAMMAR FOCUS:	Question forms

PART ONE / READING FOR MEANING

● A New School

Previewing the Reading

A.   **Prepare to read by making up a story about the pictures. Answer these questions.**

1. Who are the people? Where are they going or what are they doing?
2. What do they have to do? Why?

B. **Read the following selection quickly for important ideas.**

Rafael Becerra and his wife are new arrivals in this big city, and they need to enroll their fifteen-year-old son, Alejandro, in the local high school. Two weeks ago they moved here from a town in Arizona, so they already know about the public school system in the United States. They've learned, for example, that financial support for schools comes from state and local taxes rather than from federal funding. Because there is little federal control over education, each state has developed its own educational plan, and every school or school district has its own budgets and standards. The Becerras have many questions about Alejandro's new school.

When Alejandro and his father walked into Chatsworth High School, they were surprised at the amount of activity they saw around them. They didn't know where to go or what to do, so they felt confused. Everyone in the crowded halls seemed to be in a hurry. Finally a student showed them the way to the main office. Everyone there was busy, too, but after a while a woman behind the counter noticed the bewildered newcomers standing in the doorway. "What can we do for you?" She had to shout because the office was so noisy.

"What do I do to enroll my son in school?" said Rafael. The woman pointed to a large room across the hall.

The long line into the room moved quickly, and soon Rafael and Alejandro were sent to a small office to talk to a student counselor. "Good morning," the counselor greeted them. "My name is Ms. Taylor. How may I help you?"

When Alejandro replied that he needed to register, Ms. Taylor asked, "Have you brought the necessary documents with you? I'll need proof of age—your birth certificate or passport. Did you also bring some verification of your present address?" Then she added, "A paid utilities bill will do." Rafael gave the papers to Ms. Taylor, and she immediately made copies of them for Alejandro's cumulative file. Rafael promised to send his son's records from former schools.

After that, they filled out some registration and health forms. Fortunately, Alejandro's immunization papers were in order, so he could enroll officially in the school right away.

Next, to be able to sign up for classes, Alejandro had to take a placement exam to test his reading and writing knowledge of English. When he came to the composition part of the exam, he asked, "What is an autobiography?"

"An autobiography is a short account of your life," Ms. Taylor explained. Here is what Alejandro wrote.

Autobiography

My name is Alejandro Becerra, and I was born in Cali, Colombia, on September 29, 1973. I attended elementary school there. Three years ago we moved to Glendale, Arizona, where my uncle lives. I went to Glendale Junior High. My English still needs improvement, but I got good grades there.

We came to California two weeks ago because my father got a better job. We're living in a big apartment building in Los Angeles now.

My favorite subjects are math and science, and I also want to learn computer programming. My main interests are sports and music, so I'm going to participate in after-school activities.

Alejandro finished the test quickly. After that, Ms. Taylor asked him and his father, "Do you have any questions for me?" They had many, so the counselor set up another appointment for them the next day.

C. *Getting the Main Ideas*—Circle the letter of the correct words for each blank.

1. The public school system in the United States is _____ in every city because it is not supported by federal funds.
   a. the same
   b. different
   c. very poor

2. A typical high school in a big city is usually _____.
   a. quiet and relaxed
   b. crowded and busy
   c. small

3. To register, Alejandro and his father had to meet with _____.
   a. a student counselor
   b. teachers
   c. the school principal

4. To enroll in a public school in the United States, a new student needs to _____.
   a. speak and write English fluently
   b. get financial support from the federal government
   c. show some records and papers and fill out some forms

5. In some schools, students have to _____ before they can enroll in classes.
   a. get good grades
   b. meet budgets and standards
   c. take a placement exam

D. *Recognizing Chronological (Time) Order*—Number these events in chronological order. Put 1 before the first event, 2 before the second, and so on.

_____ There wasn't much time for questions, so the counselor set up another appointment for Rafael and Alejandro the next day.

_____ A woman in the main office directed them to a line of people across the hall, and soon they were able to see a counselor.

_____ After that, Alejandro took an English placement test and wrote an autobiography.

_1_ Rafael Becerra moved with his wife and son from Arizona to California two weeks ago.

_____ Alejandro went with his father to Chatsworth High to register, but they didn't know what to do at first.

_____ Rafael gave Ms. Taylor some of the necessary papers, she made copies of them, and he promised to send others.

_____ Next they filled out some registration and health forms.

E. Now that you have read the story, look back at the pictures on page 20 and retell it.

F. *Expressing Your Own Ideas*—To express your opinions, write *yes* or *no* before each of the following questions. In small groups, discuss the reasons for your answers. Then summarize your discussion for the class.

1. _____ Should the federal government fund and control all the schools and school districts in the country?

2. _____ Do busy, crowded schools in big cities usually have better educational plans and higher standards than schools in smaller towns?

3. _____ Are most school counselors very helpful to new students?

4. _____ Is the enrollment process at schools in this country very difficult?

5. _____ Should students choose their own class level? (Is an English placement test unnecessary?)

6. _____ Is formal education important for success in life?

PART TWO / VOCABULARY BUILDING

● More Synonyms ● More Descriptive Words ● More Parts of Speech

A. Match the words in the column on the left with the synonyms in the column on the right by writing the letters on the lines. (You can look back at the reading selection "A New School" to find the words in context.)

1. _d_ new arrivals   **a.** financial support

2. ____ enroll   **b.** register

3. ____ funding   **c.** verification

4. ____ documents   **d.** newcomers

5. ____ bewildered   **e.** papers

6. ____ proof   **f.** confused

Before or after a direct quotation (the speaker's exact words), the most common verb is *said*, but for variety most writers use other descriptive verbs.

Example:

Because of the noise the woman **shouted**, "May I help you?" (*Shouted* means "said in a loud voice.")

B. Replace the underlined words with descriptive verbs from this list. There may be more than one possibility, but try to use each of these words once.

---

answered   replied   asked   greeted   explained   added   promised

---

"Good morning," Ms. Taylor ~~said to~~ *greeted* Rafael and Alejandro Becerra. Then she said,
                              1.   2.

"How may I be of help?"

"I'd like to enroll my son in this school," said Rafael.
                                              3.

"Well, first I'll have to see the necessary papers," Ms. Taylor said. Then she said, "I'll
                                                                     4.   5.

need proof of his age."

"We have his birth certificate right here," said the father. "And we'll send you
                                               6.

records from his former schools as soon as possible," he said.
                                                              7.

"That's all right," said the counselor. "We don't need those papers immediately."
                      8.

If you know the part of speech (for instance, noun, verb, adjective, or adverb) of a new word, you may be able to guess its meaning more easily. You can often tell the part of speech from the purpose of the word and its position in a sentence.

Nouns are usually subjects or objects. They have singular and plural forms. They often appear before verbs and after *a/an*, *the*, adjectives, verbs, or prepositions.

Examples:

A young **woman** behind the **counter** finally noticed the **newcomers**.

Verbs express actions or conditions. They appear in different tense forms after subjects, before objects, and in infinitive phrases after *to*.

Examples:

They **didn't know** what to **do**, so they **asked** a student who **was walking** toward the office.

Adjectives describe nouns. They often appear after verbs of condition (*be*, *feel*, *stay*, etc.) and before nouns.

Examples:

Busy, crowded high schools seem **exciting** to newcomers.

Some adverbs are related to adjectives. They usually end in *-ly*, describe the action of a verb, and answer the questions "how?" or "in what way?"

Examples:

Fortunately, Alejandro finished the exam **quickly**.

C. On the lines, write the part of speech of each underlined word (*n* = noun, *v* = verb, *adj* = adjective, *adv* = adverb).

The Becerras are new (*adj*) arrivals (___) in this city, so they need to enroll
1.   2.

(___) their son officially (___) in the local (___) high school. When they arrived
3.   4.   5.

(___) at the school (___), they were (___) surprised at the amount (___) of
6.   7.   8.   9.

activity (___) around them. Unfortunately (___), everyone in the crowded (___)
10.   11.   12.

halls (___) seemed (___) to be (___) in a hurry (___). But Rafael
13.   14.   15.   16.

immediately (___) stopped a student who was walking (___) toward the office to
17.   18.

ask (___) directions (___).
19.   20.

> If a familiar word does not seem to make sense in a sentence, it may be
> because you have not correctly identified its part of speech. For example,
> many words can be either a noun or a verb.
>
> **Example:**
>
> We have to **move** (*verb*), but the **move** (*noun*) will be expensive.

D. For each pair of underlined words, write *n* (= noun) on the line after the noun and
v (= verb) on the line after the verb.

1. Every state makes educational plans (*n*) and plans (*v*) a budget.

2. Each school district has its own budget (____). When funds are low, school officials
   have to budget (____) carefully.

3. There was a crowd (____) in the main office, and more students began to
   crowd (____) into the hall.

4. Please don't hurry (____)! If you are in a hurry (____), you may make a mistake.

5. You need a document (____) like a birth certificate to document (____) your age.

6. The machine copies (____) papers quickly, and it makes larger or smaller
   copies (____), too.

7. Please file (____) these school records in the student's cumulative file (____).

8. Alejandro saw a sign (____) that told him where to sign (____) up for classes.

*E. To learn vocabulary, list other words from the reading selection "A New School" that
can be either nouns or verbs. Then write sentences that use the words in both ways.

*F. In small groups, list as many nouns as you can from the reading selection in three
minutes. The group with the most correct words is the winner. Repeat the activity with
verbs and adjectives.

PART THREE / SCANNING FOR INFORMATION

● School Information and Forms

> In any school situation, there is information to read and there are forms to fill
> out. For yourself or your children, you might need to read catalogs, schedules,
> notices, campus maps, etc. You may need to fill out registration forms, health
> cards, and so forth.

A. **Skim these excerpts from school schedules, maps, and forms. Circle the letters of the kinds of papers you have read or filled out before.**

A				
				19___

NAME (LAST)   (FIRST)   (MIDDLE)

GRADE   H.R.   AGE   DATE OF BIRTH   MO.   DAY   YEAR

RESIDENCE   CITY OR ZONE   TELEPHONE

PARENT OR GUARDIAN   BUSINESS ADDRESS OF PARENT

MAJOR SEQUENCE   SCHOOL LAST ATTENDED

H.R. ADVISER

PER	ROOM	DAYS	SUBJECT	SUBJECT GRADE LEVEL	TEACHER
1					
2					
3					
4					
5					
6					

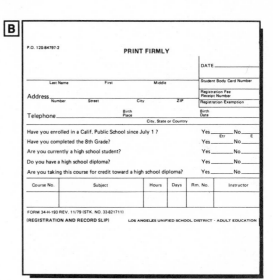

B

P.O. 12S-84797-2   **PRINT FIRMLY**

DATE____

Last Name   First   Middle   Student Body Card Number

Address_____   Registration Fee Receipt Number

Number   Street   City   ZIP   Registration Exemption

Telephone_____   Birth Place   Birth Date

City, State or Country

Have you enrolled in a Calif. Public School since July 1?   Yes____ No____
Have you completed the 8th Grade?   Yes____ No____
Are you currently a high school student?   Yes____ No____
Do you have a high school diploma?   Yes____ No____
Are you taking this course for credit toward a high school diploma?   Yes____ No____

Course No.	Subject	Hours	Days	Rm. No.	Instructor

FORM 34-H-193 REV. 11/79 (STK. NO. 33-821711)
(REGISTRATION AND RECORD SLIP)   LOS ANGELES UNIFIED SCHOOL DISTRICT · ADULT EDUCATION

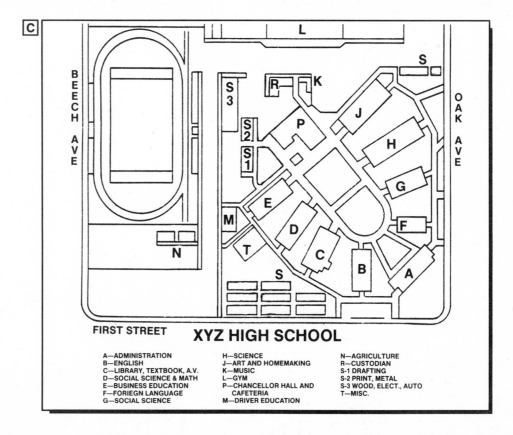

C   FIRST STREET   **XYZ HIGH SCHOOL**

A—ADMINISTRATION
B—ENGLISH
C—LIBRARY, TEXTBOOK, A.V.
D—SOCIAL SCIENCE & MATH
E—BUSINESS EDUCATION
F—FORIEGN LANGUAGE
G—SOCIAL SCIENCE

H—SCIENCE
J—ART AND HOMEMAKING
K—MUSIC
L—GYM
P—CHANCELLOR HALL AND
     CAFETERIA
M—DRIVER EDUCATION

N—AGRICULTURE
R—CUSTODIAN
S-1 DRAFTING
S-2 PRINT, METAL
S-3 WOOD, ELECT., AUTO
T—MISC.

D

CHATSWORTH HIGH SCHOOL
BELL SCHEDULE

1A - 1B BELL SCHEDULE

Per. 1A	8:00 - 8:40
Per. 1B	8:46 - 9:30
Per. 2	9:36 - 10:26
BRUNCH	10:26 - 10:40
Per. 3	10:50 - 11:34
Per. 4	11:40 - 12:24
LUNCH	12:24 - 1:04
Per. 5	1:10 - 1:54
SSR	1:54 - 2:14
Per. 6	2:20 - 3:04

E

PERMANENT SECONDARY HEALTH HISTORY (Confidential)

Medical	(Please print in pencil)	
Insurance	Family physician _____	
Yes ___	Address _____	last seen _____
No ___	Family dentist _____	
	Address _____	last seen _____

ILLNESS (past or present):

	Yes	No		Yes	No
Measles, severe			Hearing problem		
German Measles, 3-day			Vision problem		
Mumps			Speech problem		
Whooping cough			Heart disorder		
Scarlet fever			Kidney disease		
Rheumatic fever			Asthma		
Polio			Hay fever		
Meningitis			Eczema		
Encephalitis			Diabetes		
Tuberculosis — pupil			Convulsions		
— in family			Hernia		
Infectious hepatitis			Menstrual problems		
Frequent ear infections			Drug or other allergic		
" colds or sore throat			reactions		

(over)

F

CHATSWORTH HIGH SCHOOL
MAJOR DISASTER STUDENT RELEASE CARD

_____
Date

_____   _____   _____
Name of Pupil - PRINT last name first   Grade   Period 2 Teacher

Parents should indicate below the option they wish followed in the event of a major emergency in which the closing of school and immediate dispersal of pupils is imminent:

/CHECK YOUR CHOICE/

_____ 1. Leave school and go directly home or to a pre-arranged meeting place.

_____ 2. Remain at school until called for by parent or other authorized persons listed on the reverse side of this card.

Note: SCHOOL BUS RIDERS--Unless otherwise indicated above, bus riders will be transported to regular bus stops as soon as transportation is available.

_____   _____
Signature of Student   Signature of Parent/Guardian

VALID DURING ENTIRE ENROLLMENT AT CHATSWORTH HIGH OR UNTIL REVOKED
Return to Assistant Principal's Office for Release Sticker

_____ **B.** **Match these descriptions to the excerpts by writing the letters *A–F* on the lines.**

1. *E* part of a health history card

2. _____ a class enrollment slip

3. _____ a parent's instructions for major emergencies

4. _____ an individual's program card (class schedule)

5. _____ part of a campus map

6. _____ a schedule of class periods for the whole school

_____ **C.** To decide if these statements are true or false, scan the material in Exercise A. Write *T* (true) or *F* (false) on each line.

Excerpt A

1. _F_ This school has only four daily class periods.
2. _____ There is more than one grade level at this school, and students can have different teachers for different subjects.

Excerpt B

3. _____ Parents fill out this slip for their elementary school children.
4. _____ The slip will include information about a course the student is taking.

Excerpt C

5. _____ All the buildings on this campus have the names of famous people.
6. _____ Classes in the same or related subjects meet in the same building.

Excerpt D

7. _____ There is an extra class period (not numbered) before the regular school day.
8. _____ School begins in the late morning and ends in the late afternoon.
9. _____ There's a lunch break of one hour.

Excerpt E

10. _____ The school health form asks for the names of the family's doctor and dentist as well as the name of the insurance company.
11. _____ The student or parent checks the "yes" boxes if he or she has had no past diseases or health problems.
12. _____ The form says that no student who has had past diseases can attend school.

Excerpt F

13. _____ High school students need no permission to leave school at any time.
14. _____ In an emergency, the school can close and dismiss students.
15. _____ All students walk to this high school because it is close to their homes.

_____ ***D.** Discuss the meanings of any important new words and then fill out the forms (A, B, E, F) in Exercise A with information about yourself or a school-age child.

_____ ***E.** Beyond the text: Bring to class some information and forms from local schools (elementary or high schools, adult schools, city colleges, private schools, etc.). List new words and find out their meanings. From the catalogs and brochures, ask and answer questions about the schools. Fill out the forms with information about yourself or your children.

PART FOUR / EXPRESSING YOURSELF IN WRITING

● Autobiographies

> An autobiography is a personal account of your own life. When you apply to a school or for a job, you might have to or want to include an autobiography with your application.

A. *A First Draft*—To begin a short autobiography, you can follow these steps. Don't worry about grammar and other writing rules at first. Just put down your ideas as they come to mind. Leave space between lines so you can make corrections later.

1. On a piece of paper, write the answers to these questions in full sentences. Write about one page.

   - When and where were you born?
   - What were or are your parents' names and occupations?
   - Where and when did you attend school (elementary school, high school, etc.)?
   - When and why did you come to the United States or Canada?
   - Have you gone to school here before? If so, where and for what purpose?
   - Where have you worked? What did or do you do?
   - What are your interests?
   - What are your plans for the future?

2. On the back of your paper, put down one word or phrase that tells the purpose of your autobiography (**Examples:** to get a new job, to apply for financial support).

3. Reread what you wrote. Which information will not be useful in an autobiography for the purpose you chose? Cross out those sentences.

Chronological Order

Because an autobiography is a kind of history, it usually tells events in chronological order and includes some dates and time expressions. The first event comes first, the second one comes second, etc.

Example:

I was born in Cali, Colombia, on September 29, 1973, and I attended elementary school there. Three years ago we moved to Arizona. I went to Glendale Junior High. Last month we came to California.

Here are some examples of time expressions.

on Thursday	a year ago	then	soon
on October 12	last month	next	right now
in December	after that	the next day	for two weeks
in 1987	after a while	immediately	in a month

B. **Number these events in time order. Then write them in time order as an autobiography, in paragraph form. You can add time expressions like those in the above list.**

_____ I took the state law exams in the fall of 1985, but I didn't begin a law apprenticeship then.

_2_ I went to elementary school in my home town for eight years.

_____ In 1978 I passed the national high school exit exam and applied for admission to the University of Tuebingen.

_____ Now I'm planning to enroll in medical school to become a doctor.

_1_ I was born in Rottweil, Germany, on July 31, 1958.

_____ Instead, I immigrated to the United States with my American wife and our new baby.

_____ Then we moved to the city of Stuttgart, where I attended high school.

_____ After two years there, I transfered to the Free University of Berlin to continue my law studies.

_____ I needed to improve my English, so I spent the next few years in this country studying at an adult school and working.

_____ **C.** **Number the events of your own autobiography from Exercise A in time order. Then add time expressions and rewrite the autobiography in paragraph form.**

Combining Sentences (*and, but, so*)

To improve the style of your writing, you can sometimes combine short sentences into longer ones. Here are some common connecting words with their purposes.

and (adds information)   so (shows a result—the effect of a cause)
but (shows contrast)

Use a comma before these connecting words if they join two sentences with different subjects.

Example:

My main interest is computers. I'm going to learn programming. = My main interest is computers, **so** I'm going to learn programming.

_____ **D.** **Join the sentences in each of these pairs with a connecting word: *and, but,* or *so.***

1. I was born in Timor, Indonesia, on July 18, 1966. I started elementary school there.

I was born in Timor, Indonesia on July 18, 1966, and I started elementary school there.

2. In 1974 my family moved to Jakarta. I finished the fourth grade there.

3. I wanted to continue my schooling. I had to work for my family.

4. I left school at the age of ten. I had to continue learning to read and write on my own.

5. My parents wanted me to marry a rich Indonesian man. I fell in love with a Canadian.

6. He wanted to return to his country. I went with him.

Now combine some of the sentences of your own autobiography, if possible.

Writing Questions

When you write for a specific purpose (**Example:** to apply to a school), you should think about what the readers might want to know.

Examples:

> Why do you want to go to this school?
> How long do you plan to attend?
> What courses are you going to take?

E. Exchange papers with a classmate. Read your partner's purpose and autobiography. For the chosen purpose, what else do you think people would need or want to know about your classmate? List questions for him or her on another piece of paper. Give back his or her paper with your list of questions.

F. Which of your partner's questions on your autobiography were useful? Rewrite your autobiography to include the answers. Then correct your grammar, your use of punctuation, your spelling, etc. Read your paper to a small group or to the class.

*G. A biography is an account of someone else's life. To prepare to write a short biography, make a list of questions to ask. (For examples, see the questions in Exercise A on page 30.) "Interview" a classmate, friend, or acquaintance and take notes on the answers to your questions. Then, in paragraph form, write the important events of your partner's life story in time order. Combine short sentences if possible. After you correct your grammar, punctuation, and spelling, read your biography to your partner and to the class.

CHAPTER 3

Money, Money, Money

READING AND WRITING FOCUS: Business letters
Credit statements

**NEW READING AND
VOCABULARY SKILLS:**   Understanding business language
Recognizing nouns used as adjectives
Recognizing word forms (parts of speech)

WRITING SKILLS: Using connectors that introduce additional
information (*and*, *or*, *too*, *also*, *as well as*,
either, *both*)
Using business letter form

GRAMMAR FOCUS: Nouns and determiners

PART ONE / READING FOR MEANING

● A Business Loan

Previewing the Reading

A. **Prepare to read by making up a story about the pictures. Answer these questions.**

1. Who are the people?
2. What are they doing, thinking, or saying?

B. Read the following selection quickly for important ideas.

Giovanna Bevilacqua and her husband Ruggiero moved into a large apartment building soon after they arrived in this country. At home in Italy Ruggiero was the head chef of an elegant restaurant, but here he has only been able to get a job as a waiter. Giovanna also works (as a nurse's aide in a hospital), but she isn't satisfied with her work, either. The Bevilacquas are saving every penny they can to fulfill a dream of theirs. They want to open a restaurant in Los Angeles. Today a letter arrived from the bank with some information that both Giovanna and Ruggiero have been waiting for. This is what the letter said:

I.O.U. Trust and Savings Bank
1 Second Street
Los Angeles, California 90057
(213) 555-9999

May 18, 19XX

Mr. and Mrs. Ruggiero Bevilacqua
1747 Esperanza Lane, Apt. 215
Los Angeles, CA 90051

Dear Mr. and Mrs. Bevilacqua:

In response to your inquiry of May 9, we are enclosing an information sheet on our bank loan services.

We hope that this enclosure will answer most of your questions. If you need additional information, either call our loan department between the hours of 10:00 a.m. and 3:00 p.m. or visit us in person.

We look forward to having the opportunity to serve you.

Very truly yours,

Gianni J. DiVincenzo

Gianni J. DiVincenzo
Chief Loan Officer

GJD: cm

Here is the information sheet that the bank enclosed:

I.O.U. TRUST AND SAVINGS BANK
INFORMATION FOR BORROWERS

For your convenience, here are the answers to the questions that most applicants ask about our loan services.

Is it easy to get a loan? If your credit rating is good and you are earning sufficient income, your chances are favorable, especially if you are a regular client at our bank.

What do you require of your borrowers? If you are requesting a loan for business purposes, we must receive a summary of your business plan. Naturally, it is our policy to give priority to applicants with a high probability of success. Any sizeable business or personal loan requires collateral, or security for repayment of the amount borrowed, but loans for less than $2000 may be approved on the applicants' signatures alone.

How can we apply for a loan? Obtain a loan application from the nearest branch of our bank. To provide an accurate account of your individual situation, please fill out the form with a complete financial and employment history for all applicants. We will begin processing your application as soon as we receive it and will set up an appointment for a personal interview as well.

What is the rate of interest? The percentage that each borrower pays on a loan will depend on both the term of the loan and the current interest rates. These begin at 10% per year.

What is the term of the loan? The length of time allowed for you to repay a loan will depend on your individual situation. The longer the term, the higher the total interest, but a longer term permits the borrower to make smaller monthly payments.

The next day Giovanna picked up a loan application and set up an appointment for a personal interview for herself and Ruggiero with Gianni DiVincenzo. At the interview, the Bevilacquas were pleased to learn that the head loan officer came from the same town in Italy as they did. They hope that their common ethnic background, as well as their attitudes and goals, will help them to get approval for their loan.

C.   *Getting the Main Ideas*—Circle the letter of the correct words for each blank.

1. The Bevilacquas are saving and trying to borrow money to _____.
   a. fulfill a business dream
   b. go back to Italy
   c. pay off a loan

2. Chances are favorable that applicants will get a loan if _____.
   a. they offer very little money as collateral
   b. they pay interest at a lower percentage rate than usual
   c. their credit and salaries are good and they have an account at the bank

3. The amount borrowed, the rate of interest, and _____ will depend on the borrowers' individual situation.
   a. the term of the loan
   b. the items in the application
   c. the request for a financial history

4. The Bevilacquas hope that their _____ will help them to get approval of their loan application.
   a. letter-writing style
   b. ethnic background and goals
   c. former jobs

D. *Understanding Details*—For each statement write *T* (true) or *F* (false) on the line. Correct the false statements.

1. _____ If you are applying for a business loan, you must provide information about your personal life and grades in school.

2. _____ Banks prefer to lend money to applicants who will probably be financially successful.

3. _____ A sizeable loan requires three or more signatures, but only collateral is necessary for a smaller one.

4. _____ To get a loan, borrowers must fill out an application with their financial history and set up an interview.

5. _____ The rate of interest is usually the same for all situations.

6. _____ The longer the term of the loan, the higher the monthly payments but the smaller the total amount of interest.

E. Now that you have read the story with the bank's letter and information sheet, look back at the pictures on page 35 and answer the questions again.

F. *Expressing Your Own Ideas*—Check each of the following statements that you agree with. In small groups, discuss the reasons for your answers. Then summarize your discussion for the class.

1. _____ If you want to start a new business, you should use your own money. A bank loan is not a good idea.

2. _____ Most banks are eager to set up a personal relationship with clients and to serve them in any way they can.

3. _____ It is easier to get a sizeable loan if you don't really need the money.

4. _____ The bank doesn't have to ask a lot of financial and personal questions. It can trust its clients to repay their loans as they promise.

5. _____ Financially, a long-term loan is a better idea than a short-term one.

PART TWO / VOCABULARY BUILDING

● Business Vocabulary ● Nouns Used As Adjectives ● Word Forms (Parts of Speech)

> The vocabulary of business correspondence is often more formal than the words of everyday speech or stories. As an example of more formal language, in the above sentence the word *correspondence* replaces the more common word *letters*.

A. Match the business vocabulary in the column on the left with the less formal synonyms in the column on the right by writing the letters on the lines. (You can look back at the reading selection "A Business Loan" to find the words in context.)

1. _f_ fulfill		a. large
2. _____ response		b. get
3. _____ additional		c. chance
4. _____ inquiry		d. customer
5. _____ opportunity		e. letter asking for information
6. _____ client		f. satisfy
7. _____ sizeable		g. put in
8. _____ obtain		h. present
9. _____ enclose		i. answer
10. _____ current		j. more

B. Replace the underlined words with more formal words and expressions from this list.

request	sufficient	client	give priority to
require	probability	accurate	our policy
earning	favorable	complete	account

If you are <u>making</u> <u>enough</u> income, your chances of getting a loan are <u>good</u>,
          1.   2.   3.

especially if you are a regular <u>customer</u> of this bank. <u>What we usually do</u> is to <u>ask for</u> a
                                         4.   5.   6.

summary of your business plan. Of course we <u>prefer</u> applicants with a high <u>chance</u> of
                                                          7.   8.

success. We also <u>need</u> you to <u>fill out</u> an application form with a(n) <u>careful and correct</u>
                       9.   10.   11.

<u>story</u> of your credit history.
12.

> To shorten sentences, writers often use nouns as adjectives (to describe other nouns).
>
> **Examples:**
>
> an apartment building = a building with apartments in it
> a savings bank = a bank where people put their savings

_____ **C.** **Change six phrases in this paragraph so that they include nouns used as adjectives. (You can look back at the reading selection to find the answers.)**

an information sheet

The bank sent the Bevilacquas ~~a sheet of information~~ about loans from the bank for

purposes of business. It included rates of interest. Also enclosed was an application for a

loan that asked about their history of employment.

> Some words have the same form in two or more parts of speech (**Examples:** _work, dream, answer, visit, rate, bank_). But most often a word has different forms for different parts of speech.
>
> **Example:**
>
> The Bevilacquas **arrived** (_verb_) in the United States in December, and they got jobs soon after their **arrival** (_noun_).

_____ **D.** **On each line, write the appropriate form of the word in parentheses. (You can look back at the reading selection to find the answers.)**

1. Giovanna and her husband are saving money to ____ _fulfill_ ____ (fulfillment) a dream of theirs.

2. In _____ (respond) to your _____ (inquire), we are enclosing an _____ (inform) sheet.

3. Our _____ (enclose) will answer your questions.

4. What do you _____ (requirement) of a _____ (borrow)?

5. We give _____ (approve) for loans to businesses with a high probability of _____ (succeed).

_____ ***E.** **To learn vocabulary, list ten nouns from the reading selection "A Business Loan" or something else you are reading (Examples: _loan, summary_). List the corresponding verbs, if any (Examples: _lend, summarize_), and write sentences that use both forms. Repeat the activity with ten verbs and their corresponding nouns. Read your best sentences aloud to the class.**

PART THREE / SCANNING FOR INFORMATION

● Credit Statements

A. Skim this paperwork for obtaining a loan. Circle the letters of the kinds of information you have given before.

CONFIDENTIAL CREDIT STATEMENT

	SELF			SPOUSE			
Employment Income	$	p/mo. $	p/yr.	$	p/mo. $	p/yr.	A.
Commissions	$	p/mo. $	p/yr.	$	p/mo. $	p/yr.	
Dividends ☐ Interest ☐	$	p/mo. $	p/yr.	$	p/mo. $	p/yr.	
Rent from Real Estate ☐	$	p/mo. $	p/yr.	$	p/mo. $	p/yr.	
Child Support ☐ Alimony ☐	$	p/mo. $	p/yr.	$	p/mo. $	p/yr.	
Other Income	$	p/mo. $	p/yr.	$	p/mo. $	p/yr.	
TOTAL	$	p/mo. $	p/yr.	$	p/mo. $	p/yr.	

If you are self-employed, include a complete financial statement or copy of your income tax return from last year.

Type of Property	1.	2.	3.	4.	
Address					B.
Present Market Value					
Total Indebtedness					
Equity					
Annual Gross Income					
Annual Net Income					
Monthly Loan Payments					

ASSETS			OBLIGATIONS					
BANK	BRANCH		ITEM	Lender & Loan No.	Pmt Per/Mo.	Orig. Amount	Balance Due	
		$	Auto		$	$	$	
		$	Furn. & Appl.					
		$	Pers. Loans					
		$	Child Support					
Securities (See schedule attached)		$	Alimony					C.
Auto(s): Year: Make:		$						
Year: Make:		$						
Furniture and Appliances		$						
Value of R.E. Owned		$						
Net Cash Value of Life Insurance		$						
Other Assets		$						
Mortgages Owned		$	TOTAL					
TOTAL		$						

CREDITOR	ADDRESS	Amount Owed	
			D.

Ever Bankrupt?	Ever had any judgements or foreclosures?

I assure you that the above information is complete and correct. You may verify it and check my credit and employment history.

_____ Date

_____ Applicant   _____ Applicant

_____ **B.** Match these descriptions with the sections of the paperwork in Exercise A by writing the letters *A–D* on the lines.

1. ____ credit references   3. ____ family income

2. ____ real estate owned   4. ____ possessions and debts

_____ **C.** Match the vocabulary from the form in the column on the left with the explanations in the column on the right by writing the letters *a–q* on the lines.

Section A

1. _c_ spouse   **a.** money paid to one's spouse after divorce

2. ____ commissions   **b.** property (land and buildings)

3. ____ dividends   **c.** husband or wife

4. ____ real estate   **d.** payments of shares of profit

5. ____ alimony   **e.** a percentage received on sales

Section B

6. ____ market value   **f.** an estimate of the worth of property

7. ____ indebtedness   **g.** total before deduction or expenses

8. ____ equity   **h.** total amount owed

9. ____ gross income   **i.** income after deduction of expenses

10. ____ net income   **j.** the money value of property minus the claims on it

Section C

11. ____ assets   **k.** debts (money owed)

12. ____ securities   **l.** possessions with money value

13. ____ mortgages   **m.** documents that show ownership of properties (especially stocks and bonds)

14. ____ obligations   **n.** agreements about property that serve as security for repayment of loans

Section D

15. ____ creditor   **o.** legal decisions in court

16. ____ bankrupt   **p.** legally judged unable to repay debts

17. ____ judgments   **q.** a person who has lent money

18. ____ foreclosure   **r.** repossession of property because of nonpayment of debt

_____ **D.** Circle the abbreviations in the form on page 41 and tell what you think they mean.

EXAMPLES: R.E. = real estate   p/mo. = per month   Exp.= expenses

_____ **E.** Discuss the meanings of any important new words. Then fill out the form in Exercise A with information about yourself and your family.

_____ ***F.** Beyond the text: Bring to class some financial forms from local banks. List new words and find out their meanings. Fill out the forms with information about your individual situation.

PART FOUR / EXPRESSING YOURSELF IN WRITING

● Business Letters

> When it is difficult to communicate by telephone and when you want to keep records of requests, responses, and information, you can correspond in writing. The most important part of business correspondence is the body of the letter. It usually contains one to three paragraphs—an introduction, statements and questions that fulfill the purpose of the letter, and a comment on the future (usually instructions for the next step to take, an offer, a hope, or an expression of thanks).

A.
A First Draft—To begin a business letter, you can follow these steps. Don't worry about grammar and other writing rules at first. Leave space between lines so you can make corrections later.

1. Choose a real situation and purpose. On a piece of paper, write phrases to describe your financial situation (**Examples:** have never had credit, would like a credit card, don't know much about getting a loan). Then write phrases to tell the purpose of your letter (**Examples:** to find out if you are eligible for a card, to request an application form).

2. Use the phrases you wrote in Step 1 to compose the body of a letter in one to three paragraphs: you might introduce your situation, "get down to business," and comment on the future.

3. Reread what you wrote. Can you replace some everyday words and phrases with more formal language? If so, change some of your vocabulary to make your letter more businesslike.

Connectors that Introduce Additional Information

To improve the style of your writing, you can leave out repeated words and show the relationships of ideas with connecting words and phrases. Here are some common connectors to add information.

and...too	as well (as)	either...or
and...also	both...and	and...either

Use *also* in various sentence positions and *too* or *as well* at the end. *As well as* introduces an additional phrase.

Examples:

A high income helps. + A good credit rating is useful = A high income helps, and a good credit rating is **also** useful. = A high income helps, and a good credit rating is useful **as well** (= **too**).

We require a personal interview. + We require a written application. = We require a personal interview **as well as** a written application.

Use *both...and* to emphasize addition and *either...or* to express a choice.

Examples:

We'd like to meet with you. + We'd like to meet with your husband. = We'd like to meet with **both** you **and** your husband.

You can call. + You can write us a letter. = You can **either** call **or** write us a letter.

Use *and...either* to combine two negative sentences.

Example:

We don't have enough savings. + The bank won't give us a loan. = We don't have enough savings, **and** the bank won't give us a loan, **either**.

B. **Join the sentences in each of these pairs with a connecting phrase: *and...too*, *and...also*, *as well (as)*, *both...and*, *either...or*, or *and...either*. (There are several possibilities, and you may have to leave out repeated words.)**

1. In my culture, most people save their money. They believe in paying cash.
   In my culture most people save their money, and they believe in paying cash, too.

2. Some people have savings accounts. Some have checking accounts.

3. Credit cards are not very common. Store charge accounts aren't very common.

4. I've never opened a charge account. My husband has never applied for credit.

5. We don't have a credit rating. We haven't gone into debt.

6. Now my husband and I want to rent a small office. We need to buy supplies.

7. We don't have enough savings. Our relatives can't lend us money.

8. We need a loan to start our business. We have to have credit cards.

Now combine some of the sentences in your business letter, if possible.

Business Letter Form

XXXXX Xxxxxxxx Xx.	the sender's address [1]
Xxxxxx, Xxxxx XXXXX	
Xxxxxxxxxx XX, XXXX	the date [2]
Xx. Xxxxxxx Xxxxxxx	
XXX Xxxxxxxxxxx Xx.	the name and address of
Xxxxxxxxxx XX XXXXX	the receiver [3]
Dear Xx. Xxxxxxxxxxx:	the greeting [4]
Xxxxx xxxxxxxx xxxxxxxxxxxxxxx xxx xxxxxxx xxxxxxx xxxx x xxxxx xxxx.	
X xxxxxx xxxxxxxxxxxxxxx x xxxx xxx x xxxxxx xxxxxxxxxxx. Xxxxxxxxx xxx x xxxxxxxxx xxx xxxxxx x xxxxxx? Xxxxxxx x xxxxxx x xxxxxxx.	the body of the letter [5]
Xxxxxx xxxxx xx xxxxxx xx xxxxxxxxxx xxxxx xxxxxxxxxxxx.	
Yours truly,	the closing [6]
Mohammed El Gamal	the signature [7]
Xxxxxxxxxxx X. Xxxxxxxxx	the typed name of the sender [7]

[1] Your name does not belong in this return address. You can write out all words or use abbreviations with periods (**Examples:** *St., Rd., CA, NY*). If you abbreviate a state name, the U.S. Postal Service prefers the official two-letter abbreviations, without periods, listed in most telephone books.

[2] You can write out the date of the letter or use an abbreviation for the month (**Example:** *Jan.*)

[3] Put the receiver's title (**Examples:** *Mr., Ms.*) and name on the first line.

[4] Begin the greeting with a capital letter. If you know the name of the receiver, use it in the greeting. Otherwise, begin with "Dear Sir or Madam." A colon follows the greeting.

[5] Paragraphs in a business letter do not need indentation. If you don't indent them, leave a space between each one.

[6] Begin the closing with a capital letter. Another common closing for a business letter is "Sincerely (yours)." Follow the closing with a comma.

[7] Be sure to include a signature. End the letter with your typed name.

_____ **C.** Use the following information to write a business letter in the above form. Use your own name and address and today's date. If possible, type your letter.

You have heard that the Small Business Administration lends money to new businesses. In Los Angeles, California, the address of the SBA is 2007 Wilshire Blvd., L.A. 90007. You want to buy a small gas station but cannot borrow enough money from the bank because you have never owned a business before. You want to know the requirements of the SBA for small business loans, receive written information about their services, and fill out an application if you are eligible. You hope to hear from the SBA soon.

_____ **D.** Rewrite your letter from Exercise A in business letter form. (Type it, if possible.) Correct your grammar, your use of punctuation, your spelling, etc.

_____ ***E.** Exchange papers with a classmate. Read your partner's letter and write another business letter as a response.

_____ ***F.** If possible, mail your first letter. When you get a response, tell the class about it. Compare it to the answer that your classmate wrote.

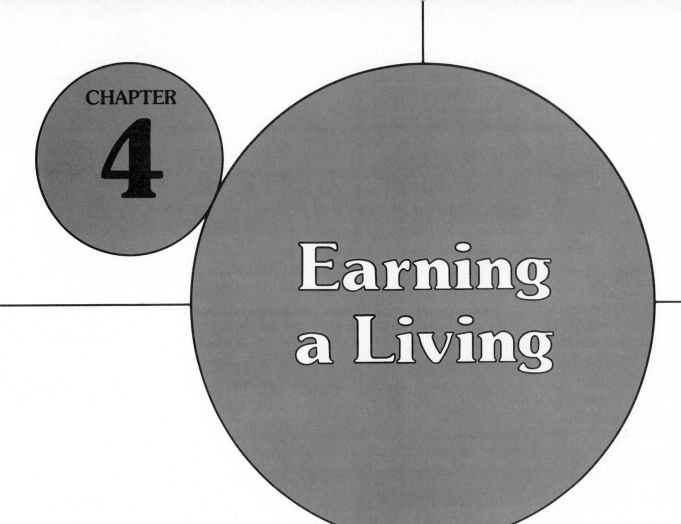

CHAPTER

4

Earning a Living

READING AND WRITING FOCUS: Letters of application
Resumes
Employment ads

**NEW READING AND
VOCABULARY SKILLS:** Judging the importance of details
Understanding "impressive" vocabulary
Recognizing related words (using the dictionary)

WRITING SKILLS: Writing concisely
Using business letter form

GRAMMAR FOCUS: Infinitives

PART ONE / READING FOR MEANING

● Advancing in the World of Work

Previewing the Reading

A. **Prepare to read by making up a story about the pictures. Answer these questions.**

1. Where are the three men?
2. What does one of the men want? How is he trying to get it?

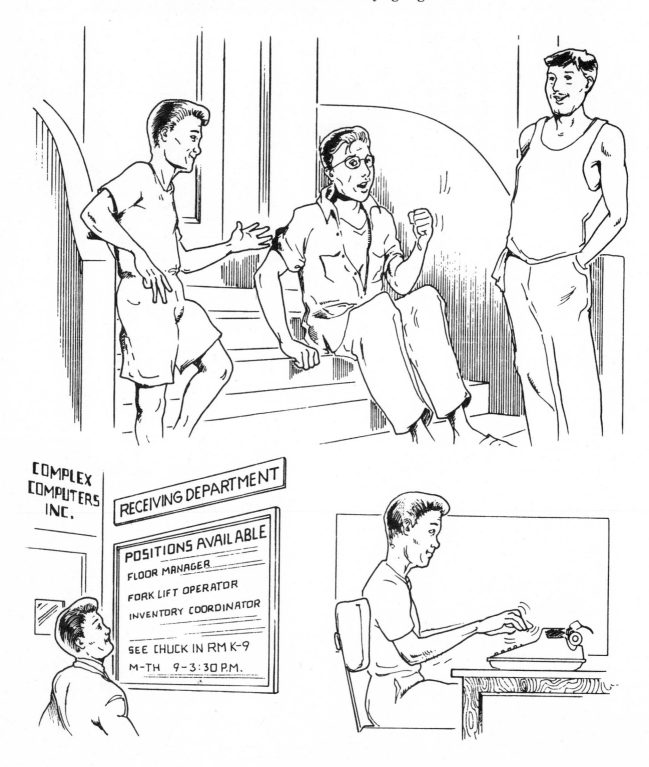

B.   Read the following selection quickly for important ideas.

One hot evening Long Trinh Dang, Rafael Becerra, and Ruggiero Bevilacqua, who were all living on the same floor of the same building, were sitting on the apartment house steps trying to cool off. They often sat outdoors together in the early evening to talk about their own countries and their work, as well as the problems they were having.

Long was telling the other two that his present salary was barely enough to cover his family's living expenses. His neighbors already knew that as a businessman in his own country, Long had the respect of many people and the power to make decisions. But when he came to this country several years ago, his English was not fluent enough, and he did not understand the world of business well enough, to take on a position of great responsibility. So he ended up with a job as the parts inspector in a computer firm. He was dissatisfied: the work was tedious, and he didn't have much opportunity to make use of either his language abilities or his technical ones. In order to be able to compete in the world of work here, Long was taking courses—not only advanced English but also business computer applications.

The next day at work, Long was surprised to see a notice on the bulletin board of his department. The announcement said:

POSITIONS AVAILABLE

In accordance with our policy of recognizing effective performance and superior achievement, we are eager to advance qualified candidates within our organization. We encourage career-minded employees to apply for the following immediate opportunities.

Position	Department
Clerk-Typist	Accounting
Sales Representative	Marketing
Computer Engineer	Research

We advise applicants to bring or send in a resume to Mr. Robert K. Ram, Personnel Director, Room 5514 (Deadline: July 30).

To impress the personnel director with his ability to communicate in English, Long decided to write a letter of application in addition to his resume. With the help of his English instructor, this is what he wrote:

1747 Esperanza Lane, #211
Los Angeles, CA 90051
July 8, 19XX

Mr. Robert K. Ram, Personnel Director
Complex Computers, Inc.
1341 Disk Drive, Room 5514
Los Angeles, CA 90046

Dear Mr. Ram:

The purpose of this letter is to apply for the position of sales representative, as announced on the bulletin board in the Receiving Department.

As a parts inspector, I enjoy being a team member of your outstanding organization but am seeking more challenging work—a position that will enable me to contribute my talents: exceptional language ability (fluency in Vietnamese and French and a good command of English), an aptitude for technical details, and excellent communication skills.

As you will see from the enclosed resume, I had the responsibility of supervising an entire sales staff in my country before I immigrated with my family to the United States. From my extensive experience in marketing, I understand sales techniques and am eager to apply them. Along with the motivation to succeed, I am confident that I have the qualifications you are seeking in a representative of Complex Computers.

You can reach me at Extension 5301. Or you can call me at home at (213) 555-6734 after 6:30. I am looking forward to the opportunity for a personal interview.

Very truly yours,

Long Trinh Dang
Long Trinh Dang

C. *Getting the Main Ideas*—Circle the letter of the correct words for each blank.

1. Long Trinh Dang was dissatisfied with his present position because _____.
   a. the work was too difficult and technical
   b. he wanted a higher salary, more respect, and more challenging work
   c. it wasn't helping him to improve his English

2. When he was living in his country, Long _____.
   a. was a businessman with power and responsibility
   b. didn't work because there was a war
   c. didn't have the opportunity to make use of his talents

3. On the bulletin board of his department the next day, Long saw a notice of _____.
   a. better positions in another computer company
   b. employees recognized for superior performance
   c. available openings within the same firm

4. To apply for a promotion, the first thing Long did was to _____.
   a. go to the personnel office for a personal interview
   b. submit a letter of application and a resume
   c. take a test in French and English

D. *Judging the Importance of Details*—On the lines, check the events in the story that were important in Long's attempt to get a promotion. Don't check the other details even if they are true.

1. _✓_ Long's job as a parts inspector wasn't challenging enough to make use of his talents.

2. ____ He was studying advanced English and business computer applications.

3. ____ The notice on the bulletin board in the Receiving Department announced openings for a clerk-typist and a computer engineer as well as a sales representative.

4. ____ The office of Mr. Robert Ram, the personnel director of Complex Computers, Inc., is in Room 5514.

5. ____ Long's English teacher helped him to write a letter of application.

6. ____ Long has had extensive marketing experience and understands sales techniques.

E. Now that you have read the story, look back at the pictures on page 48 and retell it.

F. *Expressing Your Own Ideas*—To express your opinions, write *yes* or *no* before each of the following questions. In small groups, discuss the reasons for your answers. Then summarize your discussion for the class.

1. ____ If you are dissatisfied with your position, should you talk about your work problems with friends and acquaintances?

2. ____ In any job, are the salary and benefits more important than the challenge and opportunity to make use of your abilities?

3. ____ To get ahead in the world of business, do you need both special skills and fluency in English?

4. ____ To make a good impression on a job application, is the letter you write more important than the personal interview?

5. ____ In your letter, should you exaggerate your skills and experience?

PART TWO / VOCABULARY BUILDING

● "Impressive" Vocabulary ● Related Words (Dictionary Use)

> A firm may want to impress potential employees with the benefits of working
> for the company, and a job applicant may want to impress potential employers
> with his or her talents. To give a positive impression, some employment ads
> and many letters of application contain strongly positive vocabulary that may
> be exaggerated.

A. Match the "impressive" vocabulary in the column on the left with the "less positive" words in the column on the right by writing the letters on the lines. (You can look back at the reading selection on page 49 to find the words in context.)

1. _d_ be eager   a. direct
2. ____ career-minded   b. give
3. ____ challenging   c. certain
4. ____ enable   d. want
5. ____ contribute   e. knowledge (of a language)
6. ____ command   f. make possible for
7. ____ supervise   g. concerned about work opportunities
8. ____ confident   h. difficult

B. Replace the underlined words with stronger or more positive words and expressions from this list.

recognize	organization	achievement	individuals
appreciate	second to none	seeking	environment
motivation	exceptional	talent	

organization
Our ~~company~~ is looking for above-average people with the aptitude and necessary
1.   2.   3.   4.   5.   6.

reasons to succeed in our fast-paced, competitive surroundings. We notice and
7.   8.

put a value on superior performance and offer a benefit package that is very good.
9.   10.   11.

Many words are related parts of speech with the same stem (the word part that carries the meaning) but different endings.

Examples:

I want to **succeed** (*verb*) because **success** (*noun*) is important to my family. After I complete my education **successfully** (*adverb*), I'm going to be **successful** (*adjective*) in business.

In most dictionaries, you will find related words either in the same entry or in separate ones.

_____ **C.**   **Write the correct words from the dictionary entries on the lines following the parts of speech (*n* = noun, *v* = verb, *adj* = adjective, *adv* = adverb).**

1. n: _____

   v: _____

   adj: _____

   adv: _____

ex·pend (ik spend′), *v.t.* **1.** to use up: *He expended much energy on his work.* **2.** to pay out; disburse; spend. [late ME < L *expend(ere)* (to) weigh out, lay out, pay] —**ex·pend′er,** *n.* —**Syn. 1.** consume, empty. See **spend.**
ex·pense (ik spens′), *n.* **1.** cost or charge. **2.** a cause or occasion of spending: *A car can be a great expense.* **3.** the act of expending; expenditure. **4. expenses,** *Com.* charges incurred in the execution of an undertaking or commission.
ex·pen·sive (ik spen′siv), *adj.* entailing great expense; very high-priced; costly: *an expensive party.* —**ex·pen′sive·ly,** *adv.* —**ex·pen′sive·ness,** *n.*

2. n: _____

   adj: _____

   adv: _____

flu·ent (flōō′ənt), *adj.* **1.** spoken or written effortlessly: *fluent French.* **2.** able to speak or write smoothly, easily, or readily: *a fluent speaker.* **3.** easy; graceful: *fluent motion; fluent curves.* **4.** flowing, as a stream. **5.** capable of flowing, or fluid, as liquids or gases. [< L *fluent-* (s. of *fluēns*) flowing, prp. of *fluere;* see -ENT] —**flu′en·cy,** *n.* —**flu′ent·ly,** *adv.*

3. n: _____

   v: _____

   adj: _____

im·press[1] (*v.* im pres′; *n.* im′pres), *v.,* **-pressed** or (*Archaic*) **-prest; -press·ing;** *n.* —*v.t.* **1.** to affect deeply or strongly in mind or feelings; influence in opinion. **2.** to fix deeply or firmly on the mind or memory.
im·pres·sion (im presh′ən), *n.* **1.** a strong effect produced on the intellect, feelings, or conscience, etc. **2.** the first and immediate effect of an experience or perception upon the mind.
im·pres·sive (im pres′iv), *adj.* having the ability to impress the mind; imposing; awesome. —**im·pres′sive·ly,** *adv.*

4. n: _____

   adj: _____

   adv: _____

   prep: _____

ex·cept[1] (ik sept′), *prep.* **1.** with the exclusion of; excluding; save; but: *They were all there except me.* —*conj.* **2.** only; with the exception (usually fol. by *that*): *parallel cases, except that one is younger than the other.*
ex·cep·tion (ik sep′shən), *n.* **1.** the act of excepting. **2.** the fact of being excepted. **3.** something excepted: an instance or case not conforming to the general rule. **4.** an
ex·cep·tion·al (ik sep′shə nəl), *adj.* **1.** forming an exception or unusual instance; unusual; extraordinary. **2.** unusually excellent; superior. —**ex·cep′tion·al′i·ty,** *n.* —**ex·cep′tion·al·ness,** *n.* —**ex·cep′tion·al·ly,** *adv.* —**Syn. 1.**

5. n: _____

   v: _____

   adj: _____

or·gan·i·za·tion (ôr′gə ni zā′shən *or, esp. Brit.,* -nī-), *n.* **1.** the act or process of organizing. **2.** the state or manner of being organized. **3.** something that is organized. **4.** organic structure; composition. **5.** a body of persons organized for some end or work. Also, *esp. Brit.,* **or′gan·i·sa′tion.** [late ME *organizacion* < ML *organizātiōn-* (s. of *organizātiō*) = *organizāt(us)* organized (ptp. of *organizāre;* see ORGANIZE) + *-iōn-* -ION] —**or·gan·i·za′tion·al;** *esp.*
or·gan·ize (ôr′gə nīz′), *v.,* **-ized, -iz·ing.** —*v.t.* **1.** to form as or into a whole consisting of interdependent or coordinated parts: *to organize a committee.* **2.** to systematize: *to organize the files of an office.* **3.** to give organic structure or character

D. Use the words from the dictionary entries on the previous page to fil in the blanks.

1. It's _expensive_ to live in the city, but Long's family was trying not to live _expensively_. They were _____ing a lot of energy in the attempt to cut down on _____.

2. Long was _____ in French, but he couldn't speak English _____, so he was studying to improve his _____.

3. Long's resume _____ed the director because Long's qualifications are _____. He made a good _____ during the interview, too.

4. The company usually hires native speakers for sales positions, but it made an _____ in Long's case because he seemed _____ motivated. His knowledge of sales techniques was _____, and he had experience in every kind of sales-related job _____ one.

5. A manager needs _____ ability to be able to _____ a department within an _____.

*E. To learn vocabulary, list five words from the reading selection on page 49 or something else you are reading. Do you know or can you figure out related words (nouns, verbs, adjectives, adverbs)? List them and then check your guesses in a dictionary.

Using the dictionary definitions of the related words and the dictionary examples, write sentences that illustrate their meanings.

PART THREE / SCANNING FOR INFORMATION

- Employment Ads

> If a company is new, has many openings, or has trouble attracting employees, it may place a large ad in the classified section of the newspaper. The ad will probably list the job requirements and benefits, perhaps in "impressive" language.

A.   **Skim these employment ads. Circle the letters of the ads that describe jobs you might be qualified for or interested in.**

A

ADVERTISING

CLASSIFIED TELEPHONE SALES REPRESENTATIVE

We're looking for that special individual with a "voice with a smile"—who thrives in a fast-paced environment.

We offer a good base salary plus an excellent commission program.

Candidate should have exceptional skills, type 45 wpm, excellent communication skills, good command of the English language, figure aptitude, and good organizational skills. Responsibilities include selling classified ads over the phone to private parties and businesses.

Telephone sales or applicable background desired.

If you are a team player looking for a challenging opportunity to make a contribution to our winning team, please apply M-F, 9:00 a.m.–3:00 p.m. at:

Daily News

21221 Oxnard St.
Woodland Hills
Or call
Vickie Youngman
(818) 713-3376
9 a.m.-3 p.m. for interview appt.
Equal Oppty. Employer

B

Machinist

"We must be the best at everything we do."

Mr. F.X. Marshall
President

Mr. F.X. Marshall, President of the Marquardt Company, believes that words without action are nothing more than talk. Which is why the people who work here are always encouraged to do the best in an environment where top performers are appreciated and recognized. Now's the time to discover what a difference our positive atmosphere can make in your career because immediate opportunities exist for:

DRILL PRESS OPERATORS (30) 2nd Shift

Starting pay will be $4.75 per hour plus $.27 shift differential per hour, and will require candidates to lift between 50-75 pound parts from machinery to assembly areas. We offer good stability plus an excellent benefits package including full life, medical, dental, pension and thrift plan, two weeks vacation per year, eleven paid holidays, cafeteria, employee store, recreation center, credit union, discount cards and much more.

Please apply in person Tuesday through Thursday, July 7, 8 and 9, between 9-11 am and 1-3 pm at : The Marquardt Company, 16555 Saticoy St., Van Nuys, CA 91409. Equal Opportunity Employer. Proof of U.S. Citizenship may be required.

OUR ACTIONS SPEAK.

ISC THE *Marquardt* COMPANY
MEMBER OF ISC DEFENSE & SPACE GROUP

B. **Match these descriptions with the ads in Exercise A, write the letters *A–D* on the lines.**

1. ____ a telephone sales job
2. ____ a door-to-door delivery job
3. ____ an assembly-line job
4. ____ a customer service representative

C. List the important information from the ads.

Ad A

qualifications

_____
_____
_____

_____

_____

_____

responsibilities

_____

benefits

_____

_____

Ad B

benefits

_____
_____
_____
_____
_____
_____
_____
_____

Ad C

qualifications

a college degree
a strong drive to learn
ability to work in a team

_____

benefits

learn all aspects of banking
"all the benefits you'd expect"

_____

Ad D

qualifications

_____
_____
_____
_____
_____
_____
_____

responsibilities

_____

benefits

_____
_____

D. Circle the "strongly positive" words in the job ads and tell what they mean.

*E. Beyond the text: From a local newspaper, bring to class large employment ads whose purpose is to attract many applicants. List new words and find out their meanings. Then answer the following questions.

1. What kind of company placed this ad?
2. Do you think it would be pleasant to work there? Why or why not?
3. Do you meet the firm's requirements? Why or why not?

PART FOUR / EXPRESSING YOURSELF IN WRITING

● Letters of Application ● Resumes

> The purpose of both a letter of application and a resume is to attract enough positive attention that the employer will call you to set up an interview.

A.

A First Draft—To begin a letter of application, you can follow these steps. Don't worry about grammar and other writing rules at first. Write as much as you need to, but leave space between lines so you can make corrections later.

1. From Part Three of this chapter, the classified section of a local newspaper, or a bulletin board, choose a job ad or notice that interests you. Read it carefully.

2. On a piece of paper, write the job title and the place you saw the ad or notice. List the employer's requirements and the job responsibilities. Then—next to the appropriate phrases—list the skills and experience that qualify you for the position.

3. On the back of your paper, use the phrases you wrote in Step 2 and any other necessary information to answer these questions.

   - What is the purpose of the letter you are going to write? (What position are you applying for?)
   - How did you find out about the opening?
   - Why are you interested in this position with this company?
   - What makes you especially qualified for the position (skills, special abilities, background, education, experience, motivation, etc.)?
   - What can you contribute to the company?
   - What is your availability? (When can you start work?)
   - When and how can the employer reach you to set up an interview?

Concise Writing

Business communication is usually more effective if it isn't wordy (containing a lot of unnecessary words). Also, you will impress a prospective employer with your language skills if you leave out unnecessary words and combine short sentences.

Example:

Wordy: I saw your ad for the position of clerk-typist. The ad was on page 34 of the classified ads. The ads were in the *Daily News* of July 15. I'd appreciate the opportunity to be able to fill out an application. I'd like to come in for a personal interview for the position of clerk-typist.

Concise: I'd like to apply for the position of clerk-typist, as advertised in the *Daily News* of July 15.

The correct use of punctuation can also help you to be concise. Here are some additional rules:

1. You can use commas, parentheses, or dashes to separate words of explanation from the rest of a sentence. (Commas are the most common punctuation mark, but you can use parentheses and dashes occasionally for variety.)

Examples:

On the bulletin board of his department, receiving, Long saw an ad for an opening for a sales representative.

I am fluent in two languages (Vietnamese and French).

In his country, Long had a position of responsibility—manager of an import company.

2. You can use a colon to introduce a list of items in a series.

Example:

I am taking several courses to improve my skills: advanced English, data processing, and business computer applications.

B. Shorten these paragraphs leaving out repeated words and combining the information into fewer sentences. Add punctuation if necessary.

1. This letter has a purpose. Its purpose is to submit an application for a job position. I saw an announcement of the position. It was for a telephone sales representative. I saw the notice in the classified employment section of the newspaper, *The Daily News*, on Thursday, August 3.

2. You asked for a special individual with a "voice with a smile." I am a special individual with a "voice with a smile." I also have exceptional people skills. I have the skill to deal with people effectively. I am a fast typist. I type fast—45 words per minute. I have a good command of the English language. I speak, read, and write English fluently. My organizational skills are excellent. I can organize my work very well.

3. I am available for a personal interview. I would like to come in for an interview. You can reach me at home. My number is 555-6777. You can also call my extension at work. It's Extension 511.

_____ **C.** *Business Letter Form*—Use the business letter form from page 45 of Chapter 3 and the name and address in your job ad or notice to write a letter of application. (If possible, type your letter.) For the body of your letter, pick out the important information from the answers to your questions in Exercise A. Arrange it in three or more paragraphs as follows.

1. the purpose of your letter

2. the reasons for your interest, your qualifications, and what you can contribute to the company

3. your availability

Be sure to be positive in your use of vocabulary, not to repeat unneeded words, and to combine sentences and use punctuation when necessary. Correct your grammar and spelling.

_____ ***D.** Exchange letters with a classmate. Playing the role of an employer, read your partner's letter and decide if you want to interview the letter writer. Tell your partner your decision and the reasons for it.

A Resume

There are several ways to organize a resume, but the simplest and most common way is to divide the information into categories and list the important details in reverse chronological order.

E. **Use this resume as a model to write one about yourself.**

RESUME

July 19XX

Long Trinh Dang
1747 Esperanza Lane, #211
Los Angeles, CA 90051
Telephone: (213) 555-6734   **Objective:** Sales Position

Citizenship Status: Permanent Resident (Citizen of Vietnam)

Education

1968-72   University of Saigon   Major: Business
                                          Minor: French

Experience

1986-present   Complex Computers, Inc., Los Angeles, CA
                 Receiving Department Inspector
                 Responsibilities: Verifying that parts meet specification
                                    requirements

1980-1985   Manager: Golden Import Company, Saigon
                 Responsibilities: Directing activities of all sales personnel

1974-79   Salesman: Saigon Export/Import Company
                 Responsibilities: Sales

1970-74   Stockroom Clerk: Asian Export/Import Company, Saigon
                 Responsibilities: Receiving/shipping (part-time work
                                    during university study)

References

Mr. Jackson Tuttle, Receiving Supervisor
Complex Computers, Inc.

Other references upon request

---

*F. **If you are really applying for a position, retype your letter of application and send it to the address in the ad with your resume. If you get a response, tell the class about it.**

CHAPTER 5

Getting Help

READING AND WRITING FOCUS:	Legal agreements (contracts)
NEW READING AND VOCABULARY SKILLS:	Recognizing relevant points Understanding legal vocabulary Recognizing accurate definitions (using the dictionary)
WRITING SKILLS:	Organizing written agreements
GRAMMAR FOCUS:	Perfect verb tenses (present and past, simple and continuous)

PART ONE / READING FOR MEANING

● Contracts and Lawyers

Previewing the Reading

A. Prepare to read by making up a conversation for this picture. Answer this question: What are the people probably saying?

B. Read the following selection quickly for important ideas.

Because they have a lot in common, the tenants of the second floor of 1747 Esperanza Lane have been spending quite a bit of time together, talking about their everyday concerns and problems. This evening they've been discussing the law. Long Trinh Dang's brother, Hong, has been in an accident, and Long thinks he may need legal help. Because Hong's automobile insurance covers only liability for damage to others, he may have to pay not only for his own medical expenses but also for the considerable damage to his car. Hong had claimed the other driver was at fault in the accident, but her insurance company disagrees and has refused to pay.

"I don't know what to do about it," protested Giovanna Bevilacqua, "but it seems to me there are too many lawsuits in this country. People are always threatening to sue or to take someone to court over some small dispute."

"Well, I think that the way to avoid lawsuits is to put everything in writing," said Ruggiero Bevilacqua.

"Do you mean to write a contract?" asked Long, surprised. "But I'd heard that only a lawyer can make up a legal agreement."

"Oh, maybe in complicated business matters or divorces or cases like that," explained Ruggiero. "But I've been taking a course at adult school called 'Law for the Layperson,' and I've learned that any agreement between two or more people is a *contract* and that it's a good idea to put down the points in writing to avoid misunderstandings later on. Our instructor has given us models to follow, and I've written up an agreement with the workmen who are going to add a restroom to our restaurant. I'll go get it."

Ruggiero returned in a few minutes with the first page of a neatly typed agreement.

CONTRACT FOR CONSTRUCTION WORK*

1. We, Ruggiero and Giovanna Bevilacqua, Purchasers, desire to contract with Wilfred Woodman, Contractor, to perform certain work on property located at 6000 Savory Drive, Los Angeles, CA 90012.

2. The work to be performed under this agreement (Job) consists of the following: construction of a second restroom next to the existing one. The details of materials, construction, and standards of quality are listed in Addendum A.

3. Purchasers agree to promptly reimburse Contractor for the cost to Contractor of all necessary materials.

4. In exchange for Job, Purchasers agree to pay Contractor as follows:
   (a) $2500, payable in advance.
   (b) $20 per hour for each hour of work performed, up to a maximum of 100 hours, payable at the end of the week in which the work was performed.
   (c) $2500 on completion of the work.

5. Job shall be
   (a) performed daily Monday through Friday from the hours of 8:00 a.m. to 2:00 p.m.
   (b) completed by October 1, 19XX.

6. Job shall be considered completed upon approval of Purchasers, provided that Purchasers' approval shall not be unreasonably withheld. Substantial performance in a workmanlike manner shall be considered sufficient grounds for Contractor to require payment from Purchasers.

*The language in this form is from *Make Your Own Contract*, by Stephen Elias, Nolo Press, 950 Parker Street, Berkeley, CA 94710.

"Anyway," said Ruggiero after Long scanned the agreement, "the instructor of my class is an attorney and has offered to check over this contract before we sign it."

"I'm impressed," said Long, "but I still don't know what to do about my brother's case. Before the accident, I'd seen commercials on T.V. by lawyers who seem to want more business, and I've been thinking about calling one."

"They'll cost you a fortune," protested Ruggiero.

"Maybe not," interrupted his wife. "Those attorneys might take cases on a contingency basis—I've heard them promise on T.V. that you don't have to pay a penny until your case is settled."

"I hate to disagree," interrupted Ruggiero, "but an acquaintance of mine told me he'd had to pay his attorneys a retainer of thousands of dollars before they'd even start work. In any case, most of the settlement money will go to lawyers on both sides."

"Perhaps you're right," agreed Giovanna. "Long, have you gotten in touch with the local bar association to get information or—to save money—have you contacted a legal aid group?"

"But they only accept clients below a certain income level, don't they?" asked Long, as he leaned back to make himself comfortable for a long discussion...

C. *Getting the Main Ideas*—Circle the letter of the correct words for each blank.

1. Hong Trinh Dang may need the help of an attorney because _____.
   a. there's a dispute over who was at fault in a car accident
   b. he needs to write up a complicated contract
   c. he's had a problem with the local bar association

2. Before Ruggiero Bevilacqua allowed a workman to begin adding a restroom to his restaurant, he _____.
   a. had to pass an exam on "Law for the Layperson"
   b. typed up an agreement based on a model his instructor gave him
   c. paid an attorney a retainer of $2000

3. Some good places to get information about lawyers and fees are _____.
   a. car insurance agencies
   b. T.V. commercials
   c. the bar association and legal aid groups

_____ **D.** *Recognizing Relevant Points*—To prevent later conflicts, a good written contract should contain all the important points of an agreement, but not irrelevant points. On the lines, check the kinds of information that Ruggiero included on the first page of his contract.

1. _✓_ the names of the people involved in the agreement

2. _____ the names of all the workers in the contractor's company

3. _____ the address of the place where they will do the work

4. _____ a general description of the work

5. _____ the opening and closing hours of the restaurant

6. _____ the price of all necessary building materials

7. _____ the amount of fees and the manner of payment

8. _____ the time the work will be done and the date of completion

9. _____ a way to determine that the contract has ended

_____ **E.** Now that you have read the story, look back at the picture on page 62 and retell what the people are saying.

_____ **F.** *Expressing Your Own Ideas*—Check each of the following statements that you agree with. In small groups, discuss the reasons for your answers. Then summarize your discussion for the class.

1. _____ If you've had an automobile accident, you should always contact an attorney right away.

2. _____ All laypeople (people not trained in the law) should get some legal knowledge from a class or books.

3. _____ It's an insult to put an agreement with a friend or relative in writing.

4. _____ You should avoid lawyers who advertise because they're probably not good enough to get clients in other ways.

5. _____ Attorneys who accept cases on a contingency basis usually work harder than lawyers who require a large retainer and fees.

6. _____ The local bar association will recommend only the best lawyers.

7. _____ You can't get good advice or help from a legal aid society.

PART TWO / VOCABULARY BUILDING

● Legal Vocabulary ● Accurate Definitions

> In most areas of study or experience, including the field of law, there exists specialized vocabulary for that field only or with a specific meaning in that context.

A. **Match the common words from field of law in the column on the left with the specific definitions in the column on the right. Write the letters on the lines. (You can look back at the reading selection "Contracts and Lawyers" to find the words in context.)**

1. _e_ liability
2. ___ lawsuit
3. ___ contract
4. ___ legal
5. ___ layperson
6. ___ property
7. ___ contingency
8. ___ retainer
9. ___ settlement

a. a case someone brings before a court of law

b. a binding agreement between two parties to do something

c. a legal fee paid in advance, to be deducted from future charges

d. a nonprofessional (not an expert)

e. responsibility according to law

f. a word describing a basis for payment in which the attorney gets a percentage of the amount received by the client for injury or damages

g. connected with, in accordance with, or authorized or required by the law

h. anything owned or possessed

i. an amount paid to resolve a dispute out of court

> In contracts or legal discussions, the use of vocabulary may have to be more precise and accurate than in other contexts.

B. **For each underlined word, circle the letter of the more accurate definition.**

1. The landlord is suing the <u>tenant</u> for nonpayment of rent.
   a. someone who lives in a room, apartment building, or house
   b. someone who pays rent for the use of land or space in a building

2. Hong had only liability <u>insurance</u> instead of full coverage for his car.
   a. agreement by a company to provide reimbursement for loss
   b. assurance that nothing bad will happen

3. The client agrees to <u>reimburse</u> the contractor <u>promptly</u> for the cost of all necessary materials.
   reimburse: a. pay the bills
   b. pay back the money spent

   promptly: a. without unnecessary delay
   b. at the same time as

C. For each underlined word, which definition do you find the most understandable? The most complete? Why?

1. I saw a <u>lawyer</u> on a T.V. commercial.

   law·yer (lô′yər, loi′ər), *n.*   **1.** a person whose profession is to conduct lawsuits for clients and to advise or act for them in other legal matters.

   law·yer /ˈlɔjə(r)/ *n* person who practises law, esp an attorney or solicitor.

   lawyer law′-yer *lawyers.* A person trained and licensed to handle all matters having to do with the laws.—Father hired a *lawyer* to draw up the lease for the house. The *lawyer* wrote the paper so it would be right according to the law.

2. My <u>attorney</u> will represent me in this case.

   attorney at-tor′-ney *attorneys.* A lawyer; a person given legal or lawful right to act for another person.—Grandfather had an *attorney* collect the money which was due him.

   at·tor·ney (ə tûr′nē), *n., pl.* **-neys.** a lawyer; attorney-at-law. [ME < AF *attourne,* lit., one (who is) turned to, i.e., appointed, ptp. of *attourner* to ATTORN] —**at·tor′ney·ship′,** *n.* **at·tor·ney-at-law** (ə tûr′nē ət lô′), *n., pl.* **at·tor·neys-at-law.**   *Law.* a legal agent authorized to appear before a court as a representative of a party to a legal controversy.

   at·tor·ney /əˈtɜnɪ/ *n* (*pl* -neys) **1** person with legal authority to act for another in business or law: *letter/warrant of* ∼. written authority by

*D. To learn vocabulary, list ten new words from the reading selection "Contracts and Lawyers" or something else you are reading. Look up each word in two or more dictionaries (perhaps of different sizes) and copy the definition from each that fits the word in context. Then circle the most accurate definition.

PART THREE / SCANNING FOR INFORMATION

● Written Agreements

> For the more common kinds of contracts, the parties (the people involved) may use a standard form, on which they check and fill in the specific details of their agreement. If the amount of money or value of property involved is high, or if a future dispute is possible, they may want to show the contract to an attorney before signing it.

A. Skim these shortened standard contracts.* Circle the letters of the kinds of agreements that you have seen before.

A

1. _____, Seller, hereby sells and delivers the vehicle described in
      (name)
   Clause 2 to _____, Buyer.
                    (name)

2. The vehicle being sold under this bill of sale (Vehicle) is a _____.
                                                                    (year, make, and model)
   Its body type is _____. It carries the following I.D., serial, or
   engine no.: _____. Vehicle includes the following personal property
   items: _____
   _____

3. The full purchase price for Vehicle is $_____. In exchange for Vehicle, Buyer
   has paid Seller (choose one):
   [ ] the full purchase price
   [ ] $_____ as a down payment, balance due in _____ (number) days
   [ ] $_____ as a down payment and has executed a promissory note for the
       balance of the purchase price.

4. Seller hereby warrants that Seller is the legal owner of Vehicle and that Vehicle is free of
   all liens and encumbrances except: _____.

5. Vehicle (choose one) [ ] has been   [ ] has not been   inspected by an independent
   mechanic at buyer's request.
   If an inspection has been made, the inspection report (choose one) [ ] is attached   [ ] is
   not attached   to and made part of this bill of sale.

6. Seller believes Vehicle is in good condition except for the following defects: _____
   _____

Dated: _____   Dated: _____
Signed (Seller): _____   Signed (Buyer): _____
Address: _____   Address: _____

---

*The language in these forms is from *Make Your Own Contract*, by Stephen Elias, Nolo Press, 950 Parker Street, Berkeley, CA 94710, which you can buy to get copies of many other agreements for everyday use (warranties, agreements to lease personal property, contracts with independent contractors, etc.).

LANGUAGE AND CULTURE IN DEPTH: A COMPETENCY-BASED READING/WRITING BOOK

B

1. We, _____ and _____, are joint buyers of
   (name)   (name)

   the property specified in the bill of sale executed on _____, a copy of
                                                              (date)

   which is attached to this Agreement.

2. We agree that this property shall be owned by us as (choose one):

   [ ] tenants in common in equal shares

   [ ] tenants in common in the following percentages:

   _____

   Signed _____   Dated: _____

   Signed _____   Dated: _____

C

1. For value received, I promise to pay to the order of _____
                                                              (name)

   $_____ on or before _____, at _____, with
     (amount)   (date)   (place)

   interest at the rate of _____% per year.
                            (amount)

2. I also agree that this note shall be paid in equal installments, which include principal and
   interest, of $_____ per month, until such time as the principal and interest are paid
   in full.

3. If any installment payment due under this note is not received by the holder within

   _____ days of its due date, the entire amount of unpaid principal shall become
   (number)
   immediately due and payable.

4. In the event that the holder of this note prevails in a lawsuit to collect it, I agree to pay the
   holder attorneys' fees in the amount the court finds to be just and reasonable.

   _____   _____
   Date   Location

   _____   _____
   Name of Borrower   Address of Borrower

   _____
   Signature of Borrower

B.   **Match these titles and purposes with the agreements in Exercise A by writing the letters *A–C* on the lines. Use each letter twice.**

1. _____ Joint Ownership Agreement

2. _____ Bill of Sale

3. _____ Promissory Note

4. _____ to sell a car or truck

5. _____ to lend or borrow money

6. _____ to establish that two people own the same property

C. Match the vocabulary from the agreements in the column on the left with the specific definitions in the column on the right. Write the letters *a–n* on the lines.

Agreement A

1. _*d*_ hereby
2. ____ vehicle
3. ____ down payment
4. ____ balance
5. ____ due
6. ____ liens and encumbrances

a. owing; to be paid
b. claims against property as security for debts
c. partial payment at the time of purchase
d. by means of this document
e. any means for transporting goods or passengers on land
f. amount still owed

Agreement B

7. ____ joint
8. ____ executed
9. ____ tenants in common

g. belonging to two or more people together
h. holders of undivided property interests
i. signed; carried out

Agreement C

10. ____ pay to the order of
11. ____ installments
12. ____ principal
13. ____ in the event that
14. ____ prevail

j. make payments in the name of
k. win (over someone else)
l. amount of a loan, on which interest is payable
m. if; in case
n. parts of a payment spread over a period of time

*D. Discuss the meanings of any other new vocabulary and then fill out the standard contracts in Exercise A with information about a real or imaginary agreement. (If you use any of the forms for a real agreement, you may need to leave out or add sections and to retype the agreement to make it fit your individual situation.)

*E. Beyond the text: Bring to class some legal forms from an attorney's office, a library, or a legal aid society. List new words and find out their meanings. Fill out the forms with information about your individual situation.

PART FOUR / EXPRESSING YOURSELF IN WRITING

● Legal Agreements

> It's usually a good idea to put agreements about large amounts of money,
> valuable property, or important legal rights in writing, even with friends and
> relatives. A written contract forces you to think over your agreement in detail,
> helps you to remember your original intentions, and may serve as proof if a
> dispute arises.

A. *A First Draft*—To begin to write an agreement, you can follow these steps.

1. With a partner, choose a real or an imaginary situation. On a piece of paper, write the title of your agreement (**Example:** Agreement for a Room Rental).

2. Decide which questions in the following list are relevant to your agreement. Write the answers to only those questions.

   - Who are the parties (the people involved) in the agreement? (**Example:** the Tenant and the Landlord)
   - What do the parties agree to do? (**Examples:** Landlord agrees to rent a room in his apartment for six months. Tenant agrees to pay rent on the room for six months.)
   - When do they agree to do this? (**Example:** from June 1 through November 30, 19XX)
   - What are the financial arrangements? (**Example:** Tenant agrees to pay $300 a month on the first day of each month plus 1/3 of all utility bills and all charges for his or her long-distance telephone calls.)
   - If property is involved, what is it? What condition is it in at the time of the agreement? (**Example:** bed, matress, desk; furniture in good condition, room newly painted)
   - What are the other terms of the agreement? (**Examples:** that one parking space is provided, that kitchen use is included, that no smoking is allowed)
   - What will happen in the event of a dispute? (**Examples:** that the contract will no longer be valid, that the Tenant will leave the apartment, that the losing party will pay attorneys' fees)

3. Add any additional questions of your own that are relevant to your agreement and answer them.

Clear Organization and Language

A written agreement should cover all relevant points in a well-organized form. Here is one possible arrangement of points.

(TITLE)

1. Xxxx Xxxxxx (Xxxxxx) xxx Xxxxxxxx Xxxxxxx (Xxxxxxxxxx) xxxxxxxxxx xxxxxxxx xxxxx x xxxxxxxx. Xxxxxxx xx xxxxxx xxxxxxx xxxx x xx xxx xxxxxxxxxx x xxxxxxxx.

2. Xxxxxxxx xxxxx xxxx xxxxxxxxxx xxxxxx xxxxxxxx xxxxxxxxxx xxxxxx xxxxx xxxx xxxxxxxxxxxx x xxxxxx xxx xxxxxxxxxxxxx:

  (a) X xxxxxx xxxxxx x xxxxxxx x xxxxxxx xxxxxxx x xxxxx xxxxxxxxxxx x xxxxxxx x xxxxxxx x xxxxxxx xx.

  (b) Xxxx xxxxxx xxxx x xxxxxx x xxxxxx xxxxx.

  (c) Xxxxxx x xxxxx xxx xxxxxx xx xxxxxx.

3. Xxxxxx xxxxx xxx xxxxxxxxx x xxxxx xxxxxx xxxx x xxxxxx xxx xxxxxxx xxxxxx xxxxx x xxxxxx.

4. Xxxxx xx xxxxxxxx xxxxx xxxx xxxxx. Xxxxx xxxxxx xx xxxxx:

  (a) Xxxxxx xxxxx xxxxxxxx xx xxxxxxx xxxxxx xxxxx. Xxxxxx xxxxxxxxx xxxx xx. Xxxxx x xxxxxx xxx xxxxxxx.

  (b) Xxxxxx xxxx x xxxxx xxx. Xxxxx xxxx xxxxx x xxxxxxxxx.

Dated: _____   Dated: _____

Signed: _____   Signed: _____

A written agreement does not need to contain "legal language" to be binding (legally valid). But to prevent later disputes over its meaning, its language should be very clear and complete (not open to differing interpretations).

Examples:

Unclear: We agree to share the apartment.

Clear: We agree to share Apartment # 412 at 1747 Esperanza Lane, as follows:
  (a) Each roommate will have the exclusive use of one bedroom and one bathroom.
  (b) We will share the use of the living room and kitchen equally.
  (c) Patricia Losada will have the exclusive use of the one underground parking space provided.

_____ **B.**   Write an agreement in the above form based on this information. (Use only as many numbered points and lettered subpoints as necessary.) Be sure to use language that is clear and not open to differing interpretations.

Patricia Losada wants to rent out a room in her apartment to Young Park. The owner of the apartment building has given Patricia permission to have a roommate if Patricia is responsible for all rent payments and other provisions in the lease. Both roommates will have their own bedroom and bath. Young's room is already furnished: besides carpeting and drapes, it contains a bed, a chest-of-drawers, and a dresser, all in good condition. Young will be paying Patricia $300 for her share of the rent, plus half the cost of utilities (gas and electricity). Both roommates have a car, but there is only one parking space provided for the apartment in the underground garage. Patricia works at night and sleeps during the day, so she needs peace and quiet until mid-afternoon during the week. She doesn't want anyone to smoke in the apartment. She can't pay the rent on her own, so she needs Young's contribution on or before the first day of each month. She wants to be able to get the room back for herself with a month's notice, and Young wants to be able to move out with a month's notice.

_____ **C.**   With the same partner you worked with in Exercise A, write your own agreement in the above form. (Type it if possible.) Check for clear language, and correct your grammar and spelling.

_____ ***D.**   Exchange your agreement with another pair of students. Discuss the agreement you receive by answering these questions.

1. Are all the points well organized and clearly stated (not open to differing interpretations)?
2. Are any points unnecessary? If so, which ones?
3. Are any points missing? If so, which ones?
4. Can you foresee any areas that might be the subject of future dispute? If so, how can you change the language to prevent that?

   List your comments and return them with the agreement to the writers. Revise your own agreement if necessary.*

---

* For important agreements involving large amounts
of money or property, you should get professional
advice.

CHAPTER

6

Going Places

READING AND WRITING FOCUS:	Postcards and personal letters
	Tour information
	Travel descriptions
NEW READING AND VOCABULARY SKILLS:	Recognizing reasons
	Guessing meaning from context
	Finding appropriate definitions (using the dictionary)
WRITING SKILLS:	Choosing verb forms
	Using personal letter form
GRAMMAR FOCUS:	Modal verbs

PART ONE /READING FOR MEANING

● A Visit to a Travel Agency

Previewing the Reading

A. **Prepare to read by making up a story about this picture. Answer these questions.**

1. Who are the people? Where are they?
2. What are they talking about?
3. What do you think will happen next?

B.   Read the following selection quickly for important ideas.

Today, on a particularly hot day in the city, the Becerra family received a picture postcard with a cool mountain scene on it. On the back, it read:

Aug. 1
Dear Rafael, Paulina, and Alejandro,
This must be the most beautiful spot in the world! The weather couldn't be better, the hotel is comfortable, and the view from our room can't be beaten. The food is marvelous, and we must have each put on ten pounds! But we'd better cut back on our spending or we'll come home not only fat but very poor. Hope you three will be able to take some time off and get away for a while, too.
        Giovanna and Ruggiero

The Becerras
1747 Esperanza Lane Apt. 218
Los Angeles, CA 90051

"You know," said Paulina to her husband. "The Bevilacquas may be right. We've been working so hard that we could use some time off. It would be nice to get away for a while."

"It sure would!" added Alejandro enthusiastically. "I'd like to go somewhere really special. Can we get some brochures and talk to the travel agent down the street?"

That Saturday the Becerras found themselves at the Shangra-La Tours Agency. Rafael explained to a travel agent named Eric that they'd lived in Arizona for three years before they moved to Los Angeles. "We would have liked to get to know the Southwest, but we couldn't take the time to be tourists," he said. "Now we'd like to see the scenery, visit the famous sites, have some recreation, and...well, in general we've decided we need to relax."

"No problem," smiled the enthusiastic young agent. "If you want to relax, then I wouldn't advise you to drive your own car. On your vacation, you should let someone else take over the responsibility."

"Are you telling us to take a guided tour?" asked Paulina.

"I sure am," Eric encouraged her. "Instead of worrying about road maps, gas, hotel reservations, meals, and the like, you could be leaning back and enjoying the view. And with a packaged vacation, you won't have to worry about going over your budget because you'll have paid us your major expenses in advance."

"But I don't want anyone to tell me how to spend my time," protested Alejandro.

Eric went on to say that his clients had never complained that there should have been more free time, had always enjoyed the hotels, had praised the food, had complimented the tour guides, had participated in all the planned activities, had made new friends, and....

"Excuse me," interrupted Rafael. "I may have missed this part, but...have you mentioned how much all of this fun and relaxation is going to cost us?"

"Uh...let's see now," said the travel agent, riffling through a stack of papers. "Um...including airfare, all hotels, bus transportation and a tour guide, some meals—but not tips, purchases, and incidentals, of course—the price per person is only...."

C. *Getting the Main Ideas*—Circle the letter of the correct words for each blank.

1. The Becerras ____ some neighbors.
   a. went on vacation with
   b. wrote a letter to
   c. received a postcard from

2. The vacationers advised them to ____.
   a. purchase a guided tour to the East Coast
   b. not spend a lot of money on a vacation
   c. take some time off and get away from the city

3. The Becerras got travel information from ____.
   a. a travel agent
   b. the public library
   c. their neighbors

4. Eric urged them to ____.
   a. hire an individual guide
   b. take a trip with a group
   c. drive their own car

5. The Becerras are not worried that on a packaged tour ____.
   a. the hotels will be uncomfortable and dirty
   b. there won't be enough free time to do what they want
   c. the fees paid to the travel agency might be high

D. *Recognizing Reasons*—On the lines, check the reasons that the travel agent is recommending a packaged tour. Don't check the other points even if they are true.

1. _✓_ The Becerras won't have to take responsibility for driving, so they can lean back and enjoy the view.

2. ____ The scenery and the weather in the Southwest are marvelous.

3. ____ The food will be delicious.

4. ____ The vacation must be prepaid, so there will be few unexpected expenses.

5. ____ Travelers on packaged tours don't have to pay for tips, purchases, or incidentals.

6. ____ They'll be able to meet new people and participate in group activities.

7. ____ They might choose to travel by train instead of by plane.

E. Now that you have read the story, look back at the picture on page 74 and answer the questions again.

F. *Expressing Your Own Ideas*—Check each of the following statements that you agree with. In small groups, discuss the reasons for your answers. Then summarize your discussion for the class.

1. ____ Everyone needs to take time off and get away.

2. ____ The Becerras will probably not purchase the packaged tour.

3. ____ Travel agencies are a good source of information about places to spend your vacation.

4. ____ It's cheaper to travel with a group than on your own.

5. ____ It's better not to plan a vacation in advance because you'll miss the fun of unexpected adventures.

PART TWO / VOCABULARY BUILDING

● Meaning from Context ● Appropriate Definitions (Dictionary Use)

> To understand a new word or phrase from its context, first identify the part of speech (*noun, verb, adjective, adverb*). After you figure out the general meaning of the item, look for context clues that will lead you to a more specific definition.
>
> **Example:**
>
> "Uh...you want to know the price?" The travel agent **hesitated**, riffling through his fee schedules. (*Hesitated* is a verb. Its general meaning is related to speech. The words *uh* and *riffling* give clues to its specific meaning: "showed signs of uncertainty or unwillingness in speech".)

A. **To figure out the meanings of the underlined words, answer the questions that follow each statement.**

1. The food is <u>marvelous</u>, and I've put on ten pounds.

   What part of speech is the word? _____

   Does it have a positive or a negative meaning? _____

   How do you know? _____

   What is your definition of *marvelous*? _____

2. "It would be great to get away from the city!" exclaimed Alejandro <u>enthusiastically</u>.

   What part of speech is the word? _____

   What did the speaker do in this manner? _____

   What punctuation mark does the sentence in quotation marks end in? _____

   What is your definition of *enthusiastically*? _____

3. We'd like the tour to include all of the famous tourist <u>sites</u> in the area.

   Is the word a person, a place, or a thing? _____

   Who visits them? _____   When?_____

   What is your definition of *sites*? _____

> After you have completed a reading selection, guessing the meaning of new vocabulary from context, you may want to check your guesses in a dictionary. But even small dictionaries give more than one definition for most words. You have to be sure that you have chosen the appropriate meaning of the word in the context where you found it. If the dictionary examples, they will help you to choose the correct definition.
>
> **Example:**
>
> scen·ery /ˈsinərɪ/ *n* [U] **1** general natural features of a district, e g mountains, plains, valleys, forests: *mountain* ~; *stop to admire the* ~. Cf *town scenes.* **2** the furnishings, painted canvas, woodwork, etc used on the stage of a theatre.
>
> There's beautiful <u>scenery</u> in the Southwest. (The meaning numbered 1 is the correct one for the underlined word, which names something in an area of the United States, not in the theater.)

B.   For each underlined word in these sentences, write the number of the appropriate definition from the dictionary entry. The part of speech is provided.

1. If you don't take your car on your vacation, you can lean back and let the bus driver take over the <u>responsibility</u> (n: _2_).

re·spon·si·bil·ity /rɪ'spɒnsə'bɪlətɪ/ *n (pl -ties)* **1** [U] being responsible; being accountable: *You did it on your own ∼, without being told or ordered to do it. You have a post of great ∼. I will lend you my camera if you will assume full ∼ for it*, pay me the cost of any damage or loss. **2** [C] sth for which a person is responsible; duty: *the heavy responsibilities of the prime minister.*

2. Hotel <u>reservations</u> (n: _____), meals, and the like are included in the travel package, but if you have any <u>reservations</u> (n: _____) about traveling with a group, don't sign up.

res·er·va·tion /'rezə'veɪʃn/ *n* **1** [U] keeping or holding back; failure or refusal to express sth that is in one's mind; [C] that which is kept or held back: *accept sth without ∼*, wholeheartedly, completely; *accept a plan with ∼s*, with limiting conditions; *the central ∼ of a motorway*, land dividing the two carriageways. **2** [C] (US) area of land reserved for a special purpose: *the Indian ∼s*, land for the exclusive use of the Indians. ⇨ reserve¹(5). **3** [C] (esp US) arrangement to keep sth for sb, eg a seat in a train, a passage on a steamer or airliner, a room in a hotel: *My travel agents have made all the ∼s for my journey.* ⇨

3. The travel agent riffled through a <u>stack</u> (n: _____) of pages to find the information he needed and then <u>stacked</u> (v: _____) the necessary forms on his desk.

stack /stæk/ *n* [C] **1** circular or rectangular pile of hay, straw, grain, etc usu with a sloping, thatched top, for storage in the open. **2** group of rifles arranged in the form of a pyramid; pile or heap (of books, papers, wood, etc); (colloq) large amount: *I have ∼s of work waiting to be done.* **3** (brickwork or stonework enclosing a) number of chimneys. ⇨ *smoke-∼* at smoke¹(1). **4** rack with shelves for books (in a library or bookshop). **5** number of aircraft circling at different heights while waiting for instructions to land. □ *vt* **1** [VP6A,15B] ∼ *(up)*, make into a ∼ or ∼s; pile up: *∼ hay/wood; ∼ up the dishes on the draining-board.* **2** (US) ∼ *the cards*, arrange (playing-) cards unfairly; *have the cards ∼ed against one*, be at a great disadvantage. **3** [VP6A] arrange aircraft in a ∼(5).

4. The price of the travel package doesn't include <u>incidental</u> (adj: _____) expenses, of course.

in·ci·den·tal /'ɪnsɪ'dentl/ *adj* **1** accompanying but not forming a necessary part: *∼ music to a play.* **2** small and comparatively unimportant: *∼ expenses*, additional to the main expenses. **3** ∼ *to*, liable to happen or occur: *discomforts ∼ to exploration in a wild country.* ∼**ly** /-tlɪ/ *adv* in an ∼ manner; by chance.

5. The travel agency provides a luggage <u>tag</u> (n: _____) for each suitcase that you take on the tour.

tag /tæg/ *n* **1** metal or plastic point at the end of a shoe-lace, string, etc. **2** label (e g for showing prices, addresses) fastened to or stuck into sth. **3** phrase or sentence often quoted: *Latin tags.* **4** any loose or ragged end. `**question tags**, (gram) phrases such as *isn't it, won't you, are there*, added to statements. **5** [U] game in which one child chases and tries to touch another. □ *vt,vi* (-gg-) **1** [VP6A] fasten a tag(2) to. **2** [VP14] *tag*

6. Comfort is the main <u>objective</u> (n: _____)
   when selecting your travel wardrobe, so
   be <u>objective</u> (adj: _____) in your choices.

ob·jec·tive /əb`dʒektɪv/ *adj* 1 (in philosophy) hav-
ing existence outside the mind; real. ⇨ **subjective. 2** (of persons, writings, pictures) uninfluenced by thought or feeling; dealing with outward
things, actual facts, etc uninfluenced by personal
feelings or opinions. **3** (gram) of the object(4): *the
~ case*, in Latin and other inflected languages. □ *n*
1 object aimed at; purpose; (esp mil) point to
which armed forces are moving to capture it: *All
our ~s were won.* **2** lens of a microscope or tele-
scope closest to the object being looked at. **~·ly**
adv in an ~(2) manner. **ob·jec·tiv·ity** /ˈɒbdʒek-
`tɪvətɪ/ *n* state of being ~; impartial judgement;
ability to free oneself from personal prejudice.

7. We will <u>board</u> (v: _____) our motorcoach
   at 9:00 a.m., and each group member is
   responsible for being punctual.

board² /bɔd/ *vt,vi* **1** [VP6A,15B] make or cover
with boards(1): *~ up a window; ~ (over) the
stern of a boat*, cover it with boards to make a
deck. *The floor was ~ed.* **2** (⇨ board¹(8))
[VP6A,3A,E] get, supply with, meals for a fixed
weekly/monthly, etc payment: *In a university
town, many people make a living by ~ing
students. He ~s at his aunt's/with his aunt.* **~
out**, take meals at a different place from that in
which one lives and sleeps. **3** [VP6A] get on or
into (a ship, train, bus, etc);

8. Make sure you take along an <u>ample</u>
   (adj: _____) supply of any prescription
   medicine that you require.

ample /ˈæmpl/ *adj* (-r, -st) **1** large-sized; with
plenty of space: *This new car has an ~ boot.
There's ~ room for the children on the back seat.*
2 plentiful: *He has ~ resources*, is wealthy. **3** sufficient; quite enough: *£5 will be ~ for my needs.*

C. **Find the appropriate definitions of the underlined words in Exercise A in a dictionary
and write them here.**

1. marvelous: _____

2. enthusiatically: _____

3. sites: _____

Are they similar to the definitions you wrote before? Why or why not?

*D. **To learn vocabulary, list ten new words from the reading selection "A Visit to a Travel
Agency" or something else you are reading. Look up each word in a dictionary and
write down only the definition that tells the meaning of the word in the context where
you found it.**

PART THREE / SCANNING FOR INFORMATION

● Travel Information

 A. Skim these excerpts from a packet of travel information for an organized tour. Then answer these questions: Would you like to take a group trip like this one? Why or why not?

A

Dec. 20	Depart Los Angeles 7:50 a.m. Arrive Phoenix 9:55 a.m. America West Flight #64 Nonstop service
Dec. 26	Depart Albuquerque 4:42 p.m. Arrive Los Angeles 5:35 p.m. PSA Flight #39 Nonstop service

Tour members are allowed one suitcase per person. An additional suitcase may be included for an extra handling charge. Each tour member is also allowed one piece of small hand-carried luggage. There is one Shangra-La Travel Agency luggage tag per person in the flight bag we provide. Please fill out this tag and attach it to your luggage before the tour.

B

DATES *for the nights of:*	HOTEL	ADDRESS
December 20 & 21	DOBSON RANCH INN 1 (602) 555-7000	16666 S. Dobson Rd. Mesa AZ 85202
December 22 & 23	CONTINENTAL INNS 1 (800) 555-6416	850 South River Dr. Temple AZ 86001
December 24 & 25	LA POSADA DE ALBUQUERQUE 1 (505) 555-9090	125 2nd Street, N.W. Albuquerque NM 87102

Passengers may be contacted at the above addresses.

C

Temperatures will range from the mid 40s to the high 60s. Weather will be fairly mild. Comfort is the main objective when selecting your wardrobe. Bring a sweater or an all-weather coat for cooler days, as well as a fold-up plastic raincoat in case of rain.

We would remind you that comfortable walking shoes are a must.

D

DEC. 22

8:00 a.m.   Breakfast at the hotel.

8:00 a.m.   Please have luggage ready for pickup.

9:00 a.m.   We board our private motorcoach and begin our travel through Indian country. We visit Jerome and Montezuma Castle National Monument. We stop in Sedona where there is time to shop and have lunch at Tlaquepaque, a Spanish-style complex that contains specialty shops and restaurants. Late afternoon we arrive in Flagstaff and check in for two nights at the Continental Inn.

E

On a group tour every individual is responsible for being punctual; otherwise the entire group may be unfairly delayed. Please bring a wrist watch and a travel alarm clock as hotels cannot always be relied upon for wake-up calls.

Make sure you have an ample supply of any prescription medicine you may require. If you rely on prescription eyeglasses or contact lenses, it is wise to bring an extra pair. Sunglasses are good even if you don't normally wear them.

Don't forget your camera, fresh batteries, and a supply of film. Film is available en route, but shops often run out of the more popular types and it may be more expensive than at home. Avoid disappointment!

F

For meals included in the tour, when presented with the check, sign your name, Shangra-La Travel Agency, and your room number. We take care of gratuities for meals provided by the Shangra-La Travel Agency.

For your convenience, we have opened an account in your name for personal expenses at each hotel, not included in the tour cost. Typical of these incidental charges are valet, liquor, phone, room service, doctor, etc. These charges must be paid directly to the hotel cashier.

G

Your tour director will explain our seat rotation system. Rotation takes place twice daily, once in the morning upon leaving the hotel and once after the lunch stop. This gives each member of the tour the opportunity to meet new people each day.

There will be no smoking on the coach as we travel. We make morning and afternoon stops, as well as frequent picture stops and a lunch stop every day.

B. Match these descriptions with the excerpts in Exercise A by writing the letters *A–G* on the lines.

1. _____ one day's itinerary (travel plan)

2. _____ the addresses and telephone numbers of accommodations

3. _____ instructions for the tour bus

4. _____ airline and baggage information

5. _____ weather information and clothing advice

6. _____ some things to be sure to bring along

7. _____ information about payment during the trip

_____ **C.** To decide if these answers are true or false, scan the excerpts in Exercise A and underline the phrases that give the necessary information. Write *T* (true) or *F* (false) on each line.

1. _____ The trip is by train.

2. _____ The cities of departure and arrival are in three different states.

3. _____ There is no limit on lugguage and no charge for it.

4. _____ No one can call a group member during the tour.

5. _____ The weather may be cool, so group members should bring along appropriate clothing.

6. _____ There won't be much walking, so travelers should bring dressy clothes and shoes.

7. _____ All meals (including tips) are provided at no extra charge by the travel agency.

8. _____ Not all hotel charges are included in the price of the tour.

9. _____ The tour organizers want the group members to get to know one another.

10. _____ Smoking is not permitted on the tour bus.

_____ ***D.** Beyond the text: From a travel agency, get information about an organized tour and compare it with the excerpts in Exercise A. Answer these questions.

1. Which information is similar? Which is different? How?
2. Would you like to take this tour? Why or why not?

_____ ***E.** Beyond the text: From a travel agency, get brochures that describe places you would like to visit. In small groups, discuss the brochures and then choose a place and plan an organized tour to it. Each group should choose a different place. Write a "tour packet" that includes information about transportation, hotels, tour rules, and a daily itinerary. Then duplicate your packet and distribute copies to other groups. Each group chooses the tour it prefers and tells the reason for its choice.

PART FOUR / EXPRESSING YOURSELF IN WRITING

● Travel Descriptions

> Many people who don't usually communicate in writing find time to write
> postcards and letters when they are on vacation or have moved to a new place.

A. *A First Draft*—To begin a travel or a place description, you can follow these steps.
Don't worry about grammar and other writing rules at first. Just put down your ideas
as they come to mind. Leave space between lines so you can make corrections later.

1. On a piece of paper, write the name of a place that you know well (**Example:** Arizona;
   the Rocky Mountains; Guadalajara, Mexico; the place you live now; your hometown).

2. Write phrases associated with the place (**Examples:** the Colorado River and the Grand
   Canyon, mountains and deserts, ghost towns, rodeos, barbecues, sunshine). Keep writing
   until you fill one page.

3. Reread what you have written. Divide the back of your paper into columns. At the top of
   each column, write a word or phrase for each category of phrases that you wrote in Step
   2 (**Examples:** scenery, tourist sites, the weather, food).

4. Pretend that you have recently arrived in the place you named in Step 1 and are going to
   write a letter about it to friends or relatives. In the list you organized in Step 3, circle the
   phrases for the kinds of things that you'd like to tell about and cross out the topics that
   you don't want to talk about. Add other phrases, if necessary, and circle them, too.

5. Use the phrases you circled to compose a letter, using a different paragraph for each
   category or topic.

Verb Forms

As your writing becomes more complex, the verb phrases you use will be longer because they will contain more auxiliary and modal verbs—for instance, *have been, may have,* and *should be.*

Examples:

We've **been living** (*present perfect continuous*) in Phoenix, Arizona, for over a month now. Of course we **should have written** (*past advice not taken*) you sooner but we just **haven't had** (*present perfect*) enough time. You knew we **hadn't been** (*past perfect*) able to rent an apartment before we moved here, so we'**d been staying** (*past perfect continuous*) in a hotel until we **could find** (*past ability*) the right place. We **couldn't have rented** (*past impossibility*) a better apartment! We'**ll be moving** (*future continuous*) tomorrow, so I **should be packing** (*present advice not taken*) instead of writing letters, but....

B. In this excerpt from a letter, correct the forms of the underlined verb phrases. Then, if necessary, correct the verb tense forms in the letter you wrote in Exercise A.

During the time ~~we've been lived~~ *we've been living* in the hotel, we'have have a chance to see some of
       1.   2.

the area around the city. It couldn't being more beautiful! I had been told you before we
               3.   4.

left that my husband and I has really been look forward to this move. This desert and
                   5.

mountain scenery must being the most spectacular in the country! The whole family 'd
             6.   7.

liked to learn about camping out so we can spent more time outdoors without spending a
                           8.

fortune.

Next weekend we'will be travel through Indian country. Paulo 's say that he rather
               9.   10.   11.

to go shopping in Tlaquepaque and then come home, but we might staying at an inn in
                                         12.

Sedona. We know we shouldn't to miss the town of Jerome and Montezuma Castle
                    13.

National Monument, and we 'll must take time to visit an Indian village, too. We
                     14.

would've stopping to see one on the trip out here, but there wasn't enough time.
15.

Before I came to the United States to live, I would taken an organized tour to the
                                   16.

Southwest with a group of people. I'd promise myself then that some day I'had see the
                  17.   18.

Grand Canyon again, and now it looks like we'll finally have the chance. Some new

friends from work <u>have been organize</u> a guided tour that <u>maybe be</u> cheaper than any
              19.   20.

my family and I <u>could've plan</u> for ourselves.
                21.

Personal Letter Form

The form of a personal letter is simpler than that of a business letter, and the language is usually less formal. Here is an example of personal letter form.

xxxx Xxxxx Xxxxx Xx. Xxxxxxxxxxx XX xxxxx Xxx. xx, xxxx	the sender's address[1] the date[1]
Dear Xxxxxxxxx,	the greeting[2]
X xxxx xxxxxx xxxxx xxx x xxxxxxxxxx xxxxxxx xxx xxxx. Xxxxx xxxxxxx xx. Xxxxxxxxx xx xxxxxxxx! Xxxxxxxx xxx x xxxxx xxxxxx xxxx xxxxxxxxxxx xxxxx x Xxxxxxxxxx xxx xxxxx xxxxxx xx xxxxx. X xxxxxx xxxx Xxxx xx xxxxx xxxx xxxxxx xx xxxxxxx xx xxxxx xxxx. Xxxxx xxx?	the body of the letter
Warmly, *Abbas El Maori*	the closing[3] the signature[4]

[1] Your name does not belong in the return address. If you are writing to people who know your address well, you may choose to leave out this section, too. But don't forget the date.
[2] You'll probably use a first name in the greeting. Follow it by a comma.
[3] Some other closings are "Your friend," "Affectionately," "Missing you," and "Love" or anything else you choose to write.
[4] You need only a signature on a personal letter. You don't need to type your name, too.

C. Rewrite your letter from Exercise A in personal letter form, adding a greeting, closing, and signature. Correct your grammar, punctuation, and spelling.

*D. Exchange letters with a classmate. Read your partner's letter and write another letter as a response.

*E. In small groups, read your letters aloud. From the various place descriptions, choose the one place most of your group would like to visit or live in. Tell the class your choice and the reasons for it.

CHAPTER

7

Getting along with People

READING AND WRITING FOCUS:	Personal points of view
NEW READING AND VOCABULARY SKILLS:	Recognizing reasons for a point of view Recognizing "shades of meaning" (using the dictionary) Using the yellow pages of the telephone book
WRITING SKILLS:	Using phrases of comparison Using connecting words of contrast
GRAMMAR FOCUS:	Adjectives and adverbs Comparative and superlative forms

PART ONE / READING FOR MEANING

● A Family Argument

Previewing the Reading

A. Prepare to read by making up a conversation about this picture. Answer this question: What are the people probably saying and feeling?

B.   Read the following selection quickly for important ideas.

Ruggiero and Giovanna Bevilacqua have finally been able to realize their greatest dream: they've opened a new restaurant. Although they've both been working a lot harder than they ever have before, Giovanna has been feeling much more satisfied with her life now that they're finally in business. But Ruggiero has just said that he'll be happier and a lot less worried when they've paid off their business loans. "It shouldn't take longer than a year or so to realize that goal," he explained to his wife. "And then I'll be able to hire more help in the restaurant, and you can stop working."

Giovanna was surprised. "But our bills are the highest they've ever been, and the most useful thing for me to do is to contribute my time to the business. Why on earth would you want me to stop working? For what reason?"

"Obviously, that's a ridiculous question," interrupted Ruggiero, annoyed.

"It is?" asked his wife, beginning to get irritated herself. "Then what's the silly answer?"

"Why, to start a family, of course," he told her, taken aback. "Haven't I always said that a woman's most important responsibility is to have children and take care of them?"

She was shocked. "Yes, but it would be stupid to hire another hostess for the restaurant. What for? I've made sure that we serve the best food possible for the lowest possible prices, and I keep more accurate books than you do. Why, without me, that place would be a mess, the atmosphere would be less pleasant, our expenses would be much higher...and..." Giovanna was starting to raise her voice.

"Of course you've been helping me reach my goals as well as you could, Giovanna, but surely you don't mean that you should be taking responsibility for business matters. While you've certainly been helpful, the roles of men and women aren't comparable—or even similar—to each other. I thought we'd agreed that a woman can never be as valuable in the world of work as she can as...."

"As what?" she shouted. "As just a housewife and mother?"

"Exactly!" her husband shouted back. "A career woman is neither a good wife nor a good mother. When you have children, your life can't be like a single woman's."

Giovanna paused, took a deep breath, and tried to calm down. "Even though I'd like kids some day, I'm not exactly ecstatic about the idea of staying home all the time to cook and clean and look after them. At the hospital where I used

to work, the director is a woman. The chief doctor is a woman. My supervisor was a woman. They got the best education possible so they could fulfill a purpose..."

She couldn't finish her point. Ruggiero had his coat on and was walking out of the apartment. He slammed the door angrily.

She stared at the door for a while, wishing there was someone to talk to. Then she took out a pen and stationery to write to her best friend. This is the beginning of her letter:

> Dear Lola,
>
> As I wrote before, Ruggiero and I have been working as hard as we could at our new business, and I'd thought our lives were going better than ever. But now I don't know what to think. We've just had the worst argument of our marriage. I started yelling, and he walked out the door.
>
> As I see it, we've come to this country for a new start. But evidently, my husband hasn't changed as much as I have. He's still talking like his father did about "a woman's place" being in the home. I didn't leave my country and come all this way just to fulfill the same old roles in a new environment. I'd been feeling so happy in this land of "equal opportunity" for women, but now...

Giovanna wrote and wrote, signed the letter, addressed the envelope, and walked out to the mailbox to mail it. Then she went back to the empty apartment to watch T.V. and wait for her husband to return.

_____ **C.** *Getting the Main Ideas*—Circle the letter of the correct words for each blank.

1. Giovanna had been feeling more content with her life since _____.
   a. she'd gotten a promotion to a position of more responsibility
   b. she'd decided to quit work and start a family
   c. she and her husband had started running a restaurant

2. But she was surprised to hear that Ruggiero didn't think _____.
   a. she'd be working for much more than a year
   b. her contribution to the business was less important than his
   c. they should be serving the best food possible for the lowest possible prices

3. Ruggiero left the apartment angrily because his wife _____.
   a. wasn't doing the housework or cooking well enough
   b. didn't have the same view of motherhood as he did
   c. was keeping the business records more accurately than he could

4. Giovanna wrote down her thoughts and feelings in a letter to a girlfriend because _____.
   a. Americans don't believe in the equality of women
   b. she didn't want to discuss the matter with Ruggiero any longer
   c. she was upset, and there was no one to talk to

_____ **D.** *Recognizing Reasons for a Point of View*—In a difference of opinion or an argument, the speakers usually give reasons for their points of view. On the lines, write *R* before the reasons for Ruggiero's opinions and *G* before Giovanna's points.

1. _R_ A wife should work in a family business only as long as it is financially necessary.

2. _____ The best use of a woman's time is to get an education and fulfill a purpose.

3. _____ The most important goal of a woman should be to be a good housewife and mother.

4. _____ A woman can never take as much responsibility or be as valuable in business matters as a man.

5. _____ This country is sometimes known as a "land of equal opportunity" for women.

_____ **E.** Now that you have read the story, look back at the picture on page 87 and answer the question again.

_____ **F.** *Expressing Your Own Ideas*—Circle the numbers of the statements in Exercise D that you agree with. In small groups, discuss the reasons for your answers. Then summarize your discussion for the class.

_____ **G.** In small groups, discuss your answers to these questions.

1. Should two close friends or relatives try to avoid angry arguments? Why or why not? What are some ways to avoid arguements?

2. In a family, who should take the most responsibility for the family income and finances? For housecleaning and cooking? For the children?

3. Which is better—the traditional family in which the husband and wife each fulfill clearly defined roles, or the modern family in which responsibilities and rights are not clearly defined?

4. Do people from your culture usually change their ideas or goals when they have lived in this country for a while? If so, how? Do men change more than women, or vice versa?

PART TWO / VOCABULARY BUILDING

● "Shades of Meaning" (Dictionary Use)

> Synonyms or words with similar definitions may have different "shades of
> meaning" or somewhat different uses. They may appear in different situations
> or express different degrees of the same idea.

_____ **A.** **For each group of items, write 1 on the line before the word or expression with the
strongest meaning, 2 before the next strongest, and 3 before the weakest. (You can
look back at the reading selection "A Family Argument" to find the word in context.
There may be more than one right answer.)**

1. _2_ happy
   _1_ ecstatic
   _3_ satisfied

2. ___ surprised
   ___ shocked
   ___ taken aback

3. ___ realize a dream
   ___ fulfill a purpose
   ___ reach a goal

4. ___ silly
   ___ ridiculous
   ___ stupid

5. ___ annoyed
   ___ irritated
   ___ angry

6. ___ Why on earth?
   ___ For what reason?
   ___ What for?

7. ___ important
   ___ valuable
   ___ useful

8. ___ surely
   ___ of course
   ___ obviously

9. ___ raise one's voice
   ___ shout
   ___ yell

> Some dictionaries provide synonyms for many of the entries, explaining the
> similarities and differences among them. Some synonyms can appear in
> exactly the same contexts, but others can't.

_____ **B.** **List the synonyms from these dictionary entries. Then choose the better word of each
word pair in the context of the sentences that follow.**

1. great = _____

   _____

   _____

   _____

—**Syn. 1.** immense, enormous, gigantic, huge, vast, grand.
GREAT, BIG, LARGE refer to size, extent, and degree. In
reference to the size and extent of concrete objects, BIG is
the most general and most colloquial word, LARGE is somewhat more formal, and GREAT is highly formal and even
poetic, suggesting also that the object is notable or imposing:
*a big tree; a large tree; a great oak; a big field; a large field;
great plains.* When the reference is to degree or a quality,
GREAT is the usual word: *great beauty; great mistake; great
surprise;* although BIG sometimes alternates with it in
colloquial style: *a big mistake.* LARGE is not used in reference to degree, but may be used in a quantitative reference: *a
large number (great number).*

The Bevilacquas have finally realized their [greatest/most enormous] dream: to
open a [vast/big] restaurant in the middle of a [grand/huge] city. They've had to pay
a [big/large] number of bills and have made a few [big/grand] mistakes so far, and
the amount of work ahead of them is [gigantic/enormous].

2. surprise = _____

_____

_____

_____

_____

_____

_____

—**Syn. 1.** SURPRISE, ASTONISH, AMAZE, ASTOUND mean to strike with wonder because of unexpectedness, strangeness, unusualness, etc. To SURPRISE is to take unawares or to affect with wonder: *surprised at receiving a telegram.* To ASTONISH is to strike with wonder by something unlooked for, startling, or seemingly inexplicable: *astonished at someone's behavior.* To AMAZE is to astonish so greatly as to disconcert or bewilder: *amazed at his stupidity.* To ASTOUND is to so overwhelm with surprise that one is unable to think or act: *astounded by a sudden calamity.* **10.** amazement, astonishment.

Giovanna was only a little [surprised/astounded] that her husband wanted her to stop working, but she was absolutely [surprised/astonished] at his attitude toward women in the world of business.

3. argument = _____

_____

_____

_____

_____

—**Syn. 2.** ARGUMENT, CONTROVERSY, DISPUTE imply the expression of opinions for and against some idea. An ARGUMENT usually arises from a disagreement between two persons, each of whom advances facts supporting his own point of view. A CONTROVERSY or a DISPUTE may involve two or more persons. A CONTROVERSY is an oral or written expression of contrary opinions, and may be dignified and of some duration: *a political controversy.* A DISPUTE is an oral contention, usually brief, and often of a heated, angry, or undignified character: *a violent dispute over a purchase.*

Giovanna and Ruggiero have just had the worst [argument/controversy] of their married life, over an issue that has caused a great deal of social [dispute/controversy].

_____ *C.   **To learn vocabulary, list five common words from the reading selection "A Family Argument" or something else you are reading. Look up the words in a dictionary and write down several synonyms for each, if possible. If the synonyms have exactly the same meaning, write one sentence to illustrate their meaning. If they have somewhat different meanings, write several sentences to illustrate the differences.**

PART THREE / SCANNING FOR INFORMATION

● The Yellow Pages of the Telephone Book

> If you are having relationship problems that you can't seem to solve by yourselves, you may want to get professional help. If you don't know who to turn to, you can look for information in the yellow pages of the telephone book, first in the index and then in the ads and listings.

A. Where might you look for help in the following situations? Scan this excerpt from the index to the yellow pages and write the page numbers on the lines.

1. _973_ Your relationship with your young teenage daughter is getting worse and worse and you don't know how to talk or listen to her. You need advice.

2. _____ The most annoying thing about your boyfriend or girlfriend is that he or she smokes almost constantly, and you can't stand it. He or she has been trying as hard as possible to stop but can't seem to.

3. _____ You are a woman who would like more female friends and acquaintances. You'd also like to join a women's referral service for business and work purposes.

4. _____ As a result of financial difficulties, stress, and other problems, you and your spouse have been communicating less and less, and your arguments have gotten more and more serious. You don't want to break up your marriage, but you feel you need to talk to someone.

5. _____ Although you and your spouse have tried as hard as you can to solve your relationship problems, you realize you're headed toward divorce. You want the process to be as painless and fair as possible, so you're seeking a counselor to help you work out an agreement, perhaps along with an attorney.

Counselors
See Specific Kinds Such As
Alcoholism Information & Treatment Centers............44
Birth Control Information Centers...................285
Career & Vocational Counseling 332
Crisis Intervention Service.......451
Divorce Assistance..............506
Drug Abuse & Addiction Information & Treatment Centers...................532
Human Services Organizations....718
Marriage, Family & Child Counselors.................850
Mental Health Services..........866
Mental Retardation & Developmentally Disabled Services...................867
Parents Guidance Instruction.....973
Psychologists.................1148
Rehabilitation Services.........1196
Smokers' Information & Treatment Centers.........1333
Social Service Organizations.....1333
Social Workers.................1334
Spiritual Consultants...........1340
Suicide Prevention Counselors...1367
Women's Organizations & Services...................1566

B. Match these yellow-page ads with the descriptions on the next page by writing the letters *A–D* on the lines.

1. _A_ a phone number to call to get the name and number of an appropriate psychologist, therapist, etc.

2. _____ a general counseling service for all kinds of marriage and family problems

3. _____ a place for couples to get help in resolving specific issues or disputes

4. _____ a number to call to hear recorded advice

_____ **C.** To decide if these statements are true or false, scan the ads in Exercise B and underline the phrases that give the necessary information. Write *T* (true) or *F* (false) on each line.

Ad A

1. _F_ A referral service charges a fee for each name and number that it gives out.

2. _____ Couples can get counseling at this center before their marriage, and individuals can get career advice.

Ad B

3. _____ To hear advice, you can call the telephone number in the ad and ask for a tape by letter and number.

4. _____ The tapes listed are about hypnosis, sex therapy, and alcohol and drug problems.

Ad C

5. _____ A twenty-year-old therapist runs this association.

6. _____ There are twenty-five different places where you can consult with members of this organization.

Ad D

7. _____ These psychotherapists try to help couples avoid divorce.

8. _____ They accept medical insurance and claim that their charges are low.

_____ ***D.*** Beyond the text: In the yellow pages of your local telephone book, look in the index under "Counseling." Compare the kinds of services with the list in Exercise A. Then look at some of the ads and compare them with the ones in Exercise B. Discuss new words and tell what you think each kind of service offers. You may want to call one or more of them to request brochures on what they do.

PART FOUR / EXPRESSING YOURSELF IN WRITING

● Personal Points of View

A.

A First Draft—To begin to express a point of view, you can follow these steps. Don't worry about grammar and other writing rules at first. Just put down your ideas as they come to mind. Leave space between lines so you can make corrections later.

1. On a piece of paper, write a *yes/no* question about an issue of personal importance to you (**Example:** Should a father play the same role in his children's lives as the mother does?).

2. Divide the rest of the paper into two columns, with the headings Yes and No. In each column, write phrases to support the point of view above. **Examples:**

<table>
<tr><td>Yes</td><td>No</td></tr>
<tr><td>● both parents equally responsible for having child</td><td>● mother: greater role in childbearing</td></tr>
<tr><td>● child: needs both parents</td><td>● father: busy making a living</td></tr>
<tr><td>● father: teaches children valuable lessons—independence and strength</td><td>● child: needs primary caretaker—one parent more important</td></tr>
</table>

3. Circle the point of view (Yes or No) with the greater number of or the stronger arguments. Cross out the weaker supporting points in that column and add stronger ones if you can.

4. On another piece of paper, use the phrases in the column you've chosen to write your personal point of view. Write one argument or group of related arguments in each paragraph.

Comparison

You can compare various things, people, or ideas in several different ways. Here are some examples of comparative words and phrases.

	Before Nouns	**After Linking Verbs** (*be, seem,* etc.)
Likeness	Both parents play **(exactly) the same** roles. They have **similar (equal, comparable)** responsibilities.	A father's role seems to be **the same as (like)** a mother's. Their responsibilities are **similar (equal, comparable)**.
Difference	Each parent plays a **(totally) different** role. They do **unequal** work.	A father's role is **(quite) different** from a mother's. His work isn't **equal (similar, comparable)** to hers.

as Adjective/Adverb as	**Adjective/Adverb + -er than** $\begin{matrix} \text{more} \\ \text{less} \end{matrix}\Big\}$ **Adjective/Adverb than**
I'm working **as hard as** I can (work). My job isn't **as important as** my home life.	I'm working **harder than** (I ever did) before. My home life is **more important than** my job.

the Adjective/Adverb + -est

$\begin{matrix} \text{the most} \\ \text{the least} \end{matrix}\Big\}$ Adjective/Adverb

We're trying to fulfill our **greatest** dream of all.

What's **the most useful** contribution that I can make?

We serve **the best** food possible at **the lowest** possible prices.

B. Fill in the blanks with comparative words and phrases from the list. (There are many possibilities, and you can change a sentence to the negative form, if necessary.)

(un)like	comparable (to)	the same (as)	more…than	as…as
equal (to)	similar (to)	different (from)	less…than	

1. Family relationships in this country and in my culture are _____.
2. In this country, husbands and wives seem to play _____ roles.
   They have _____ responsibilities.
3. In my culture, a woman's work is _____ a man's.
4. A man's value in the business world is _____ a woman's.
5. I believe that a man's time at home is _____ important _____ his work.

C. In this expression of opinion, correct the underlined phrases. Then, if necessary, correct the comparative and superlative phrases in the point of view you wrote in Exercise A.

If a couple divorces, I feel that they should share custody of their children. The

mother and father should try <u>as hard</u> they can to reach <u>the reasonablest</u> agreement
　　　　　　　　　　　　　1.　*as* ∧　　　　　　2.

possible—even under the <u>more difficult</u> circumstances. Even if the former marriage
　　　　　　　　　　　　3.

partners refuse to speak to each other any <u>more it</u> is necessary, the children have the
　　　　　　　　　　　　　　　　　　4.

right to see each parent <u>as oftener as</u> or even <u>more oftener as</u> they did before the
　　　　　　　　　　　5.　　　　　　　6.

separation. Obviously, each situation is <u>more different</u> from every other, so every couple
　　　　　　　　　　　　　　　　　7.

will have to work out the <u>most good</u> solution—the one <u>most appropriater</u> to their
　　　　　　　　　　　8.　　　　　　　　9.

circumstances.

Connecting Words of Contrast

To improve the style of your writing, you can sometimes combine short sentences into longer ones. A clause of contrast can appear at the beginning or end of a sentence.

Examples:

While he wants a family, she's planning a full-time career. = He wants a family **whereas** she's planning a full-time career.

Although she wants children, she intends to keep working. = She intends to keep working **even though** she wants children.

D. Join the sentences in each of these pairs with a connecting word or phrase of contrast: *while, whereas, although, even though.* (There are several possibilities for some sentences, and you may want to change the order of the given pairs.)

1. Some couples fight a lot. Others seem to get along fine.

   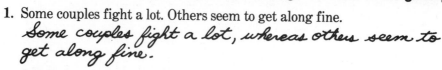
   Some couples fight a lot, whereas others seem to get along fine.

2. Arguments can be beneficial to a relationship. Silence can be harmful.

3. Some partners express their feelings openly. Others keep them inside.

4. It can damage a relationship to shout a lot. There has to be a way to express anger.

5. Couples who love each other should try to communicate. There could be some difficult problems.

6. Partners who fight may be able to work out their difficulties. In some cases they might need professional help.

E. In the paper you wrote for Exercise A, combine some of the short sentences of contrast into longer ones, if possible. Then correct your grammar, punctuation, and spelling.

*F. Summarize the point of view of your paper in a few sentences for the class. Then give it to a classmate who would like to express the opposite point of view. He or she writes a contrasting paper.

In small groups, read aloud the two points of view. Decide which paper is the stronger one and summarize your discussion for the class.

CHAPTER

8

Having Fun

READING AND WRITING FOCUS: Fliers
Instructions (games and recipes)

**NEW READING AND
VOCABULARY SKILLS:** Recognizing the order of steps in instructions
Recognizing and understanding idioms
  (using the dictionary)

WRITING SKILLS: Arranging information to attract attention
Arranging steps in instructions
Using connecting words of time order

GRAMMAR FOCUS: Gerunds and verb complements

PART ONE / READING FOR MEANING

● A Neighborhood Celebration

Previewing the Reading

A. **Prepare to read by making up a story about the pictures. Answer these questions.**

1. What probably happened before this story began?
2. Who are the people? What are they doing? Why?
3. What will probably happen after this story ends?

B. Read the following selection quickly for important ideas.

Su Yen Dang, Long's wife, was looking forward to throwing a party—a potluck picnic for everyone in the apartment complex on Esperanza Lane. She had been listening to Paulina Becerra talk about getting to know her coworkers and classmates when the idea came up. With her husband, their three small children, and her brother-in-law to pay attention to, Su Yen had been so busy taking care of the household that she hadn't taken the time to make friends of her own. But now she was really getting excited about making party plans with her neighbor.

"Here's an idea," began Su Yen enthusiastically. "What would you think of calling our party an 'international celebration'? We can start by designing a flier as an invitation." After thinking it over, this is what they came up with:

FOOD!

COLD DRINKS!

Potluck Picnic
1747 Esperanza Lane

ATTENTION ALL TENANTS

• *International Celebration* •
Potluck Picnic

All you guys, gals, husbands, wives, and the children, too!

Everyone come to the potluck picnic—
forget all your troubles and cares.
For just one day, let's all share
your country's food and drink.

Where: Pinetree
When: Sept. 5
12:00 to 6:00 p.m.

Hong Trinh Dang and friends will provide the music

Please call Su Yen Dang or Paulina Becerra for more information
and to say what you will bring
(Telephone: 555-3215)

Soccer!

Songs!

Dancing!

Games for Kids!

"I'll take care of getting the decorations," volunteered Su Yen. "But for entertainment, can we count on the teenagers in the building to provide their favorite music?"

"I'm sure we can," laughed Paulina, thinking of her son, Alejandro, whom she couldn't get to turn off his radio in their apartment. "And I suppose the older kids will keep busy dancing or talking or something. They might even feel like organizing a soccer or a baseball game. But how about planning some activities for the younger ones—and perhaps the adults, too—to break the ice? Look—here's a typical American game I copied from a library book:"

How to Have a Scavenger Hunt

Having an outdoor scavenger hunt (a traditional children's party game) is always fun, but you need to prepare for it ahead of time. First of all, write and duplicate a list of items for the players to find—the older the kids, the more difficult (unusual) they can be. It might be fun to arrange the items in reverse order of difficulty. Here are a few suggestions:

1. a leaf from an oak tree
2. a small, smooth, red rock
3. a twig longer than ten inches
4. a clean, empty, undented Coca-Cola can
5. a newspaper job ad
6. an old tennis ball
7. a 1975 penny
8. a Superman comic book
9. something in French

To begin the game, have the players divide into teams. Then hand each group a copy of the list. After making sure that they understand the object of the game (to collect all the items as quickly as possible), announce a time limit (probably an hour for a list of 8-12 items) and let the kids have a go at it.

After ending the game, score each team's collection by counting each correct item as one point. Or try scoring the number of points that corresponds to the number of each item on the list (**Example:** an oak leaf = 1 point; the tennis ball = 6 points). The winners, of course, are the team with the highest score, and you can add excitement by giving out prizes.

"Sounds great to me," agreed Su Yen. "Let's plan on spending more time at the library to get a few more ideas for games. But I'm more interested in talking about the food now. Will it be difficult to get each family to bring a different dish?"

"Not at all," Paulina said. "The American neighbors I know will prefer sharing in the party preparations. And I can't stand having one or two hostesses do all the work. Our friends from other countries love cooking, too, and I'm sure they'll enjoy tasting so many different kinds of food."

"And by sharing one another's food, we'll learn about some new dishes ourselves," added Su Yen. "I'll bet we'll have a great combination of special foods from many countries and collect some new recipes to try. I'm looking forward to meeting a lot of interesting people, getting to know the neighbors, making new friends, hearing some music, playing games, and having a great time! And maybe there will be a lot more parties after this one!"

C. *Getting the Main Ideas*—Circle the letter of the correct words for each blank.

1. While listening to Paulina Becerra talk about her new friends, Su Yen Dang got the idea of _____.
   a. having a picnic in the park for all the neighbors
   b. paying more attention to her husband and brother-in-law
   c. joining a club so that she could meet new people

2. Su Yen and Paulina decided to invite guests _____.
   a. by sending out invitations
   b. by telephoning everyone
   c. by designing and distributing a flier

3. Some of the entertainment they were planning on offering was _____.
   a. square dancing and folk singing
   b. cartoon movies
   c. music, sports, and party games

4. They weren't worried about preparing the food for so many people because _____.
   a. they'd hired professionals to do the cooking
   b. it was a potluck party, and each family would bring a dish
   c. the party wasn't at dinnertime, so the refreshments would be simple snack food

D. *Understanding Details*—Write *T* (true) or *F* (false) on each line and correct the false statements.

1. _____ Su Yen and Paulina wrote the information about the party on a flier to serve as an invitation.

2. _____ They're planning on holding the party at Esperanza Park one evening at the beginning of summer.

3. _____ It will be a picnic for children and adults of all ages.

4. _____ The guests are all going to bring music from their countries, but they'll be relying on the hostesses to provide food.

E. *Putting Steps in Instructions in Order*—Number the steps in these instructions in chronological order. Put 1 before the first step, 2 before the second, and so on.

Instructions for a Scavenger Hunt

_____ Set a time limit and start the game.

_____ Have the players divide into teams and distribute the lists.

_____ Score the number of items that each team has collected.

_____ Give the members of the winning team prizes.

_____ Write and duplicate a list of items.

F. Now that you have read the story, look back at the pictures on page 100 and retell it.

G. *Expressing Your Own Ideas*—In small groups, discuss your answers to these questions. Then summarize your discussion for the class.

1. What kind of party have you given? (What was its purpose? How did you plan it? What kind of food and entertainment did you have? Who did you invite?)
2. Would you rather be the host (hostess) or a guest at a party? Why?
3. What makes a party successful?

PART TWO / VOCABULARY BUILDING

● Recognizing and Understanding Idioms (Dictionary Use)

> An idiom is a phrase with a meaning different from the meanings of the individual words in it. To understand an idiom, you need to know the nonliteral (unusual, unexpected, or figurative) meaning.

A. **For each of these pairs of sentences, check the one that contains an idiom.**

1. ✓ Let's <u>throw a party</u> at the park.

     ____ Let's <u>throw a ball</u> at the park.

2. ____ I <u>came up</u> to your apartment to talk about our party.

     ____ I liked the idea as soon as it <u>came up</u>.

3. ____ Children sometimes <u>count on</u> their fingers when doing math.

     ____ Can we <u>count on</u> you to bring the music?

4. ____ A party game may help <u>break the ice</u>.

     ____ Let's <u>break the ice</u> into small pieces for the drinks.

5. ____ I was so tired after giving the party I <u>couldn't stand</u> up.

     ____ I <u>couldn't stand</u> doing all the work by myself.

B. **Replace the underlined words with idioms from this list.**

make some friends	break the ice	feel like
looking forward to	ahead of time	count on
have a go at	come up with	get to know

looking forward to

I'm ~~anticipating~~ the party with pleasure! I hope I'll <u>find out about</u> the neighbors and
   1.   **2.**

<u>form some friendships</u>. I've <u>thought of and offered</u> a few ideas for games to <u>make the</u>
3.   **4.**   **5.**

guests feel comfortable. At least the kids will <u>try</u> them. I can probably <u>rely on</u> the
                                          6.   **7.**

teenagers to provide their own entertainment, but I still want to make plans <u>in advance</u>
                                                                        8.

in case they don't <u>have an interest in</u> dancing or talking.
                        9.

> Some dictionaries include idioms and common phrases. To find them, look up the most important word in the idiom or phrase and look at the phrases in bold type within the entry. Some common words appear in many different expressions.

C. Circle the letters of all the idioms and expressions with the word *take* that make sense in each blank.

1. Su Yen and Long Trinh Dang aren't able to ____ this summer, so they're going to entertain guests instead.

   a. take a step to
   b. take a vacation
   c. take a trip
   d. taken aback
   e. take time off
   f. take a deep breath

2. Su Yen likes to ____ planning a party.

   a. take responsibility for
   b. take someone to court
   c. take care of
   d. take a ride
   e. take time
   f. take place

D. From this dictionary entry, list six of the many idioms and expressions that include the word *take*. Then make a sentence with each that illustrates its meaning.

1. _____ 3. _____ 5. _____
2. _____ 4. _____ 6. _____

take something out (a) remove: *have one's appendix taken out.* (b) obtain; procure (something issued): *take out an insurance policy, take out a library book* **take somebody out** conduct, accompany: *take someone out to dinner (i.e., at a restaurant)* **take it out on somebody** direct one's anger, disappointment, etc. toward something or somebody else: *She took out her anger on her children.* **take to something** (a) adopt as a practice or hobby, as a means of livelihood; get into a habit: *take to fishing when one retires; take to drink(ing); take to the road:* become a tramp (of a circus, etc.); go on tour from town to town giving shows (b) *take refuge in:* use as a means of escape; *take flight:* run away **take something over** assume control of: *He took over his father's business.* **take something up** (a) lift up, raise; (b) engage in (something) (as a hobby, business, etc.): *take up hiking, camping* (c) pursue further, begin afresh (something left off, something begun by somebody else): *He took up the job at the point where he had left off.* (d) occupy (time, space): *This piano takes up too much space. My time is fully taken up with work.*

*E. To learn vocabulary, choose a common word (Examples: *after, ahead, come, break, forward, like, place*) and look it up in a dictionary. List the idioms and expressions that contain that word, their definitions, and an example for each that illustrates its meaning.

PART THREE / SCANNING FOR INFORMATION

● Instructions (Games)

> If you are not used to entertaining, you can get advice or look through books about planning a party: making invitations, putting up decorations, preparing special food, etc. If you provide a relaxed and friendly atmosphere, the guests may have no trouble making conversation, getting to know one another, and having a good time. But in case they are quiet and shy at first, you could suggest a few "ice-breakers" (party activities to make people feel comfortable). In the right mood, many adults will enjoy playing traditional party games.

A. Skim these game descriptions. Circle the letters of the ones you might enjoy playing.

A

Because this is such a silly game, even adults seem to have a good time playing it. It's best for a large group of people. After dividing the guests into teams with an equal number of players (8-12 is ideal), have them line up behind their team leaders. Give each leader an orange. At a signal each leader places the orange under his or her chin and turns to the next person in line. Then, without touching it with the hands or dropping it, the second player somehow takes the orange under his or her chin. Next, he or she passes it to the third player in the same way, and so on. If the orange falls on the floor, the person who was passing it picks it up and starts again. The game continues until one team has managed to get the orange to the end of the line by passing it from player to player in this ridiculous manner.

B

Playing this game in a large group is more difficult than playing it in smaller ones. Again, the players stand or sit in a line. The person at one end of the line starts the game by whispering a short message—once only—to the second player. (Before beginning, you might wish to provide the first player with a funny message on a slip of paper, such as "He who laughs last, laughs best." or "Did you know that Su Yen Dang is such a perfect hostess that she's talked to every man at the party so far?") The second player whispers it to the third, and so on down the line until it reaches the other end. Finally, the last player says what he or she has just heard, and you can count on it being a lot different from the original message. You can keep the guests laughing if you ask them to repeat what they thought they heard in reverse order, starting with the second-to-last player.

C

Some people have to work at playing this popular pantomime game well, while others seem to have a natural talent for it. The object is to act out a phrase in front of your team members without speaking, so that they guess it as quickly as possible. The teams should be equal in size. To start, each team meets separately to write a number of phrases—the titles of movies, books, advertising slogans, famous quotes, idioms, or the like—each on a slip of paper. Second, the host or hostess collects the folded slips, putting them into a box or hat. Third, one player of each team in turn picks one (replacing any phrase written by his or her own team). He or she tries to pantomime it—word by word or syllable by syllable—in front of his or her team members. (Experienced players know certain gestures for providing shortcuts in this game.) By timing each attempt (and setting a time limit), the host or hostess can record the total number of minutes and seconds that each team needed to complete its phrase. When everyone has had a turn, the winning team is the one with the lowest total time score.

D

Setting up this game requires a deck of cards, which the host or hostess deals out face down to all the players sitting in a circle. First of all, players should resist showing any emotion as they look at their cards silently, especially the player receiving the ace of spades, the "murderer" card. Next, as you sit quietly and smile at one another, this "murderer" will try to kill everyone in the group by winking at them without getting caught. If someone winks at you, you have to wait quietly for ten seconds before telling the group, "I'm dead," and withdrawing from the game. The game ends when someone discovers the murderer, but catching this killer isn't easy. If you think you've seen someone wink at another player, ask the victim, "Are you dead?" and accuse the suspect only if the victim answers "yes."

_____ **B.** Match these titles with the game descriptions in Exercise A by writing the letters *A–D* on the lines.

1. _____ Charades

2. _____ Telephone (Gossip)

3. _____ Murder

4. _____ Pass the Orange

_____ **C.** Summarize the games in Exercise A by listing the steps in the instructions in order.

Game A

1. *Divide into teams of 8-12.*

2. _____

3. _____

4. _____

5. _____

6. _____

Game B

1. _____

2. _____

3. _____

4. _____

5. _____

6. _____

Game C

1. _____

2. _____

3. _____

4. _____

5. _____

6. _____

Game D

1. _____

2. _____

3. _____

4. _____

5. _____

6. _____

_____ ***D.** Choose a game from Exercise A and play it in class or at a party. Then tell the class, in steps, what happened.

_____ ***E.** Beyond the text: Get a book of games from a bookstore or the school or local library. Choose one you like, explain it to the class, and have the class play it. Then describe what happened in steps.

PART FOUR / EXPRESSING YOURSELF IN WRITING

● Fliers ● Instructions

> To notify a group of people about a planned event, you might want to design a flier as an announcement.

A. To design a flier, you can follow these steps.

1. As a class, decide on a future event, preferably one you are really planning (**Examples:** an end-of-term party, a picnic and soccer game, an international festival, a play).

2. In small groups, list phrases that describe the event (**Examples:** the purpose; the place; the time, day, and date; things to bring; the planned activities).

3. In the list you wrote in Step 2, circle the phrases that will be most important in attracting attention to the event. Copy these in larger letters.

4. Correct your grammar and spelling. Then cut apart the phrases you printed in Step 3 and arrange them on a clean piece of paper in a logical, attractive way. You can tape the phrases to the paper or copy the arrangement on another piece of paper, making necessary changes.

5. After each group shows its flier to the class and explains the reasons for its arrangement of information, the class chooses the best flier and duplicates it to distribute to people invited to the event.

> In planning a party or other social event involving many other people, you might need to write out a set of instructions about how to do something. The instructions must be clearly organized in chronological order, simple to follow, and complete.

B. *A First Draft*—To begin to write a set of instructions, you can follow these steps. Don't worry about grammar and other writing rules at first. Just put down your ideas as they come to mind. Leave space between lines so you can make corrections later.

1. On a piece of paper, write a possible title. Your title can begin with "How to...." (**Examples:** How to Play Musical Chairs; How to Make Fruit Punch.)

2. List the materials necessary (**Examples:** the items used in the game, the equipment and ingredients for the recipe).

3. List the steps in the process (exactly what to do) in chronological order.

4. Cross out any steps you listed in Step 2 that are not important, and add any missing ones. (It is important to be complete in giving instructions so that the people following them don't make any mistakes.)

Expressions of Time Order

You can use expressions of time order to make the sequence of steps in a process clear. Here are some common connecting words.

first	next	before		(Noun)	when	
second	then	while	}	(Verb*ing*)	as soon as	} (Clause)
third	finally	after	}	(Clause)	until	}

C. Add connecting words from the above list to this set of instructions and make any necessary changes. Then make the same kinds of additions and changes to the instructions you wrote in Exercise B.

How to Make Spicy Fried Chicken

Cut up a 2½ pound chicken into serving pieces. Mince a clove of garlic. Heat a frying pan over a high flame. Add a tablespoon of oil and spread it around. Fry the chicken with the garlic for about 15 to 20 minutes. Turn the pieces so they get crispy on all sides. Add salt and pepper to taste and MSG if you wish. Put the pieces on a serving platter. Sprinkle the dish with red pepper flakes, peanuts, Chinese (or regular) parsley, and green onions.

D. Correct the grammar, punctuation, and spelling of the instructions you wrote. If they are for a game, read them to your classmates so they can play it. It they are for a recipe, give them to a classmate so he or she can try it. If others can follow your instructions correctly, you will know that you have been communicating effectively.

CHAPTER 9

The Media

READING AND WRITING FOCUS:	Short essays T.V. schedules
NEW READING AND VOCABULARY SKILLS:	Recognizing the organization of points Recognizing the meanings of word parts (prefixes, stems, and suffixes)
WRITING SKILLS:	Writing general statements for essays Writing topic sentences for paragraphs Outlining Using connecting words (*furthermore*, *in addition*, *however*, etc.) and punctuation (semicolons)
GRAMMAR FOCUS:	The passive

PART ONE / READING FOR MEANING

- The Benefits of the Mass Media

Previewing the Reading

A. **Prepare to read by making up a story about the pictures. Answer these questions.**

1. Who are the people?
2. What are they doing and why?
3. In the second picture, what is he writing?

_____ **B.**   Read the following selection quickly for important ideas.

Alejandro Becerra's high school English class had been having a discussion about the mass media. Mr. Ireland, the instructor, had summed up their points of view by saying, "It's clear, therefore, that we have all been influenced by television, movies, radio, magazines, newspapers, and the like in different ways—some of them positive and some negative."

The homework was to write a short, well-organized essay on either the positive or the negative ways that people are affected by the media. After talking to a few classmates and family members and doing some research at the library, Alejandro planned and typed his paper; he also got help in correcting and revising it from a tutor at his school's learning center. This is the essay that he handed in to his English teacher.

The Benefits of the Mass Media

Every day, we are all influenced by the mass media (television, movies, radio, magazines, newspapers, and the like). Although some critics of the media claim that these means of communication are used primarily to control our thinking and get us to buy products that we don't need, the media also contribute to keeping people informed. In other words, while dangers do exist, the benefits of the media far outweigh the disadvantages. Most of the messages brought to viewers, listeners, and readers are designed either to inform or to entertain—and neither of these goals can be considered dangerous or harmful.

If consumers of the media could be taught at an early age to examine messages critically—i.e., to think carefully about what is being communicated—they would be able to take advantage of the information and enjoy the entertainment without being hurt by it. The key to critical thinking is recognizing the purposes of the news or script writers, the advertisers, and so on. Are both sides of an issue being presented? Is the amount of violence and killing shown necessary to the point of a story? Have enough facts about a product being advertised been presented?

Furthermore, in a country with a democratic form of government, the people can be kept informed by the mass media. To be able to express their views and vote intelligently, citizens need the opportunity to hear news, opinions, and public affairs programming. Information about current events is presented in depth on publicly funded T.V. channels and radio stations as well as in newspapers. In addition, the public broadcasting media can help viewers and listeners to complete or further their education. Recent immigrants, for example, can improve their command of English through T.V. and radio, and, in addition, some college courses are taught on educational television.

Another recognized advantage of the media is that it gives people the information they need in their daily lives: weather and traffic reports are good examples. While commercials and advertising do not necessarily present accurate information, they do make people aware of the availability of products that could improve their lives. In addition, they create a larger demand for some items, which may lead to a reduction in their price.

While the media can be a valuable means of educating the public, when most people turn on the T.V. set or the radio, they want to be entertained. As a result, most programming consists of movies, plays, music, comedies, game shows, and sports events. Some of these offerings are of low quality, but, on the other hand, many are fun to watch and interesting, written and presented well.

Even though the mass media can be misused, most of its effects are positive. We are all influenced by television, movies, radio, magazines, and newspapers, and—if we are careful to examine their messages critically—these can all be of benefit to our lives.

---

4. He claims that the two main purposes of the media are to _____.
   a. control our thinking and get us to buy useless products
   b. educate viewers and listeners in current events and English
   c. inform and entertain people

C. *Getting the Main Ideas*—Circle the letter of the correct words for each blank.

1. For a homework assignment for English class, Alejandro Becerra wrote _____.
   a. a paper on the negative effects of television
   b. an essay on the advantages of the mass media
   c. a description of a process

2. Alejandro's main point was that _____.
   a. the benefits of T.V., radio, and so on outweigh the dangers
   b. television is more useful as a means of entertainment than to provide information
   c. advertising is harmful when it doesn't present accurate facts

3. Alejandro feels that consumers of the mass media should be taught at an early age to _____.
   a. turn off the T.V. set when a ridiculous program comes on
   b. buy the products advertised in commercials so that the demand increases
   c. think critically about the messages they are viewing, hearing, or reading

4. He claims that the two main purposes of the media are to _____.
   a. control our thinking and get us to buy useless products
   b. educate viewers and listeners in current events and English
   c. inform and entertain people

D. *Recognizing the Organization of Points*—In Alejandro's six-paragraph essay, each paragraph has a different purpose or focuses on a separate topic. Number these six topics in the order that the corresponding paragraphs appear in his paper.

_____ the practical information the media offers for daily lives

_____ the entertainment value of T.V. and radio

_____ taking advantage of the media's benefits through critical thinking

_____ the informative and educational value of the broadcast media

_1_ the introduction to the essay

_____ the conclusion (summary of the main points)

E. Now that you have read the story and Alejandro's essay, look back at the pictures on page 112 and answer the questions again.

F. *Expressing Your Own Ideas*—Check each of the following statements that you agree with. In small groups, discuss the reasons for your answers. Then summarize your discussion for the class.

1. _____ Alejandro will get a good grade on his essay because it is well organized and contains a lot of supporting detail for his point of view.

2. _____ The positive effects of the mass media outweigh the negative ones.

3. _____ Because viewers may not be well educated, television is more effective in controlling their thinking than in informing them.

4. _____ Most commercial T.V. programming is of low quality—not worth wasting time on.

5. _____ Educational and publicly funded broadcasting is boring.

PART TWO / VOCABULARY BUILDING

● The Meanings of Word Parts (Prefixes, Stems, and Suffixes)

Suffixes (word endings) often indicate the part of speech of a word. Like prefixes (word beginnings), suffixes can also give clues to the meaning of a vocabulary item. A stem (the main part of a word) sometimes has a clue to the meaning, too. If you know the meanings of the word parts (some dictionaries include them among the entries), you may be able to figure out the meaning of a new word. Here are the meanings of a few common word parts:

Prefixes	Stems	Suffixes
ad- = forward	a(d)vant- = before	-ed = acted upon
co- = with; together	bene- = well	-er, -or = one who
dis- = not (negative)	cog- = know	
ex- = from; out of	commun- = share	-ence = condition of
in- = in; into	dem(ocrat)- = people	-ful = full of
mis- = badly; wrong	flu- = flow	-ize = to cause; to become
re- = back; again	ver- = turn	-ly = like (manner)
super- = over	vi(se)- = see	-ment = the result of

Examples:

co|work|er = one who works together with someone

   a. together   **b.** work   **c.** one who

re|verse = change direction; make into the opposite

   a. back   **b.** turn

A. Draw lines to divide each of these words into parts (a prefix, stem, and suffix, if possible). Then write the meanings of the parts that you find in the above lists. Make up a definition for the word. (You can check your definition in the dictionary.)

1. in|flu|ence = *the condition of having power over*

   a. *into*   b. *flow*   c. *the condition of*

2. revise = _____

   a. _____   b. _____

3. recognize = _____

   a. _____   b. _____   c. _____

4. dishonestly = _____

a. _____ b. _____ c. _____

5. misused = _____

a. _____ b. _____

_____ **B.** Use the meanings of the prefixes, stems, and suffixes on the previous page to make up definitions for these words. Then write the correct word from the list in each blank.

disadvantages	supervised	advance
entertainment	democratic	harmful
benefits	critically	express

In a country with a ___*democratic*___ government, the _____
                        1.   2.

of the mass media should outweigh the _____. On the other hand, if
                                        3.

children rely on television for all of their _____, it can be
                                             4.

_____ to their physical health and minds. Ideally, a child's T.V.
5.

viewing should be _____ by his or her parents, who should check the
                   6.

program schedule in _____. In addition, children should be taught to
                     7.

think about T.V. programs _____ as well as to _____
                           8.   9.

their opinions about what they have seen.

_____ ***C.** To learn vocabulary, list ten words containing prefixes or suffixes from any reading selection in this book or something else you are reading. Divide each word into parts and try to figure out the meanings of each part (prefix, stem, or suffix) by listing other words with the same part and trying to discover what their meanings have in common. You might also look up the word parts in a large dictionary. After writing your own definitions of the words, check your guesses in the dictionary. Then write a sentence with each of the words to illustrate its meaning.

PART THREE / SCANNING FOR INFORMATION

● T.V. Schedules

> As more and more network and cable T.V. channels are added to the selection that viewers can choose from, T.V. watchers have a larger choice of programs to tune in to. Most newspapers provide daily and weekly T.V. schedules with brief program descriptions in advance.

A. Scan this T.V. schedule and circle the names of the programs you have seen before. Tell the class what kind of shows they are.

Channel	8:00	8:30	9:00	9:30	10:00	10:30	11:00	11:30
②	Scarecrow and Mrs. King		Simon & Simon		Twilight Zone		News	Night Heat
③	Our World (CC)		Heart of the City (CC)		20/20 (CC)		News	Nightline
④	The Cosby Show (CC)	Family Ties (CC)	Cheers (CC)	Molly Dodd	L.A. Law		News	The Tonight Show
⑤	Movie: Massacre at Central High ('75) ★★★ (Andrew Stevens, Derrel Maury)				News Fishman, Leek		Taxi	Tales From Darkside
⑦	Our World (CC)		Heart of the City (CC)		20/20 (CC)		News	Nightline (CC)
⑨	$100,000 Pyramid	Chance of a Lifetime	News Lawrence, Gordon		Dating Game	SCTV	Carol Burnett	Wild, Wild West
⑪	News	Current Affair	Movie: Hercules in New York ('70) ★ (Arnold Schwarzenegger, Arnold Stang)				The Late Show	
⑬	Movie: Fighting Back ('82) ★★ (Tom Skerritt, Patti LuPone)				News Malloy, Rutledge		Star Trek	
⑱	NHK News	KTE News	News (9:10)	Poo Reun ...	Il Yo Il	Ae Junj ...	KTE News	Free Korea
㉒	Off the Air						Off the Air	
㉘	Nature of Things		Mystery! Sherlock Holmes (CC)		First Among Equals		American Playhouse A Case of Libel (CC)	
㉚	W.V. Grant	Evangelism	Dr. Gene Scott					
㉞	Senorita Limantour		Esa Muchacha/Ojos Cafe		Noticiero	Estampas	Cine Las Fuerzas Vivas	
㊵	Praise the Lord		Praise the Lord		Behind	J. Wimber	Larry Lea	Hal Lindsey
㊻	Home Shopping Club (6)				Home Shopping Club			
㊿	Blake's 7 Trial		Britain's Top Guns	Sneak Previews	Austin City Limits		Business Report	Computer Chronicles
㊗	La Intrusa		Cine Los Jinetes de la Bruja				Noticias	Jason King
㊶	Sport/King	H. Sheldon	Crook	Flip Side	Mod Squad		Mr. Ed	Heart
㊾	Soapbox	T. Brown	Pochtian	Off the Air				
㊿	Movie: The Harvey Girls ('46) ★★★ (Judy Garland)				News		CNN News	Movie: Johnny Apollo

B. You may be able to tell what a T.V. show is about from the title. Make guesses about the contents of some of the programs in the above schedule, and write the numbers of these categories in the appropriate boxes.

1. current events
2. drama (theater)
3. foreign language

4. comedies
5. religion
6. game shows

7. violence or horror
8. science fiction
9. mysteries or detective (police) shows

______ C. Using the schedule on the previous page, write a plan for watching T.V. from the hours of 8:00 p.m. to midnight.

8:00	10:00
8:30	10:30
9:00	11:00
9:30	11:30

______ D. In the following excerpt from a T.V. magazine, find and read the descriptions of the the programs you listed in the above plan. Do you still want to watch the same shows? If not, change your choices by crossing out some shows and writing down others. Explain your decisions to the class.

8 P.M.

② **Scarecrow and Mrs. King** Lee and Amanda search for an environmentalist whose knowledge of the Washington, D.C., water-system could be deadly in the hands of enemy agents. (R)
③⑦ **Our World** Summer, 1944. Allied forces storm the beaches at Normandy; the first USO show; women go to work in the factories. (R) (CC)
④ **The Cosby Show** Denise has difficulty being supportive of her soon-to-be-married pregnant friend. (R) (CC)
⑤ **MOVIE** "Massacre at Central High"★★★ *(R)*
⑨ **$100,000 Pyramid**
⑪ **News** "Brandwynne, Cox"
⑬ **MOVIE** "Fighting Back"★★ *(R)*
⑱ **NHK News** (In Japanese)
㉘ **Nature of Things** Computer technology in automobile design and the problems of energy and land pollution.
㉚ **W.V. Grant**
㉞ **Pobre Senorita Limantour**
㊵ **Praise the Lord**
㊿ **Blake's 7** "Trial" The abortive attack results in a court martial in Space Command Headquarters.
(52) **La Intrusa**
(56) **Sport of Kings**
(58) **Soapbox** "S-E-X" Teenagers discuss sex education, contraceptives and what they tell their parents.
(63) **MOVIE** "The Harvey Girls"★★★

8:30 P.M.

④ **Family Ties** Manager Alex attempts to change Jennifer's rock group into a swing band. (R) (CC)
⑨ **Chance of a Lifetime**
⑪ **Current Affair**
⑱ **KTE News** (In Korean)
㉚ **Christian Evangelism**
(56) **Harvey Sheldon**
(58) **Tony Brown's Journal** "NFL 28, Blacks 0" The lack of black coaches.

9 P.M.

② **Simon & Simon** Rick's long-suppressed Vietnam agony surfaces upon hearing of the murder of the medic who saved his life there. (R)
③⑦ **Heart of the City** Kevin becomes involved with Robin's alcoholic chemistry tutor; Wes has to contend with cop killers. (R) (CC)
④ **Cheers** Jilted Woody refers to Sam's black book to find a date. (R) (CC)
⑨ **News** "Lawrence, Gordon"
⑪ **MOVIE** "Hercules in New York"★ *(G)*
⑱ **KTE Guide** (In Korean)
(9:10) ⑱ **KBS News** (In Korean)
㉘ **Mystery!** "Sherlock Holmes: A Scandal in Bohemia" Holmes (Jeremy Brett) and Watson (David Burke) match wits with an opera star intent on blackmailing a king. (CC)
㉚ **Dr. Gene Scott**
㉞ **Esa Muchacha de Ojos Cafe**
㊵ **Praise the Lord**
㊿ **Britain's Top Guns** "Sailor: Happy Birthday"
(52) **Cine** "Los Jinetes de la Bruja" (1956) Kitty de Hoyos, Fernando Almada.
(56) **Crook & Chase**
(58) **Pochtlan**

9:30 P.M.

④ **Days and Nights of Molly Dodd** Fred calls Molly up on stage to sing with his band.
⑱ **Poo Reun Hae Ba Ra Gi** (In Korean)
㊿ **Sneak Previews**
(56) **On the Flip Side**

10 P.M.

② **Twilight Zone** A reform-school inmate finds true love with the warden's daughter; a middle-aged couple meet younger incarnations of themselves.
③⑦ **20/20** A Tennessee pearl farmer who is posing a serious threat to the Japanese pearl industry. (CC)
④ **L.A. Law** Van Owen's boss questions his wounded employee's will to prosecute; Brackman indulges himself with a new toupee. (R)
⑤ **News** "Fishman, Leek"
⑨ **Dating Game**
⑬ **News** "Malloy, Rutledge"
⑱ **Il Yo Il Bam Eul Dae Haeng Jin** (In Korean)
㉘ **First Among Equals** A prostitute threatens Raymond with blackmail; Simon goes into debt; Charles is offered a difficult job; a General Election is called.
㉞ **Noticiero Univision**
㊵ **Behind the Scenes; Religion**
㊻ **Home Shopping Club**
㊿ **Austin City Limits** Grammy-winner Glen Campbell ("Gentle on My Mind," "Southern Nights"); songwriter Eddy Raven ("Thank God for Kids," "Who Do You Know in California?").
(56) **Mod Squad**
(63) **News** (R)

10:30 P.M.

⑨ **SCTV** Game show "Meet the Pawnbroker"; The Flaming Turkey.
(10:35) ⑱ **Ae Junj Ui Jogun** (In Korean)
㉞ **Estampas de Mexico**
㊵ **John Wimber**
(63) **CNN News**

11 P.M.

② **News** "Schubeck, Toyota"
③ **News** "Insley, Elliott"
④ **News** "Lange, Morrison"
⑤ **Taxi**
⑦ **News** "Moyer"
⑨ **Carol Burnett & Friends**
⑪ **The Late Show**
⑬ **Star Trek** "Charlie X"
⑱ **KTE News**
㉘ **American Playhouse** "A Case of Libel" (CC)
㉞ **Cine** "Las Fuerzas Vivas"
㊵ **Larry Lea**
㊿ **Nightly Business Report**
(52) **Vea Noticias**
(56) **Mr. Ed**
(63) **MOVIE** "Johnny Apollo"★★★

11:30 P.M.

② **Night Heat** (R)
③⑦ **Nightline** (CC)
④ **The Tonight Show**
⑤ **Tales From the Darkside**
⑨ **Wild, Wild West**
⑱ **Free Korea Network**
㊵ **Hal Lindsey**
㊿ **Computer Chronicles**
(52) **Jason King**
(56) **Heart of the Nation**

*E. Beyond the text: As a class, discuss a local T.V. schedule or magazine and agree on a program to watch during a class hour (or have someone videotape a program at home for later viewing in class).

Before watching the show, answer these questions: Why did the program you chose seem interesting? (What do you think it will be about? What is its value to you?)

During the show, take notes on the events or points so that you can ask questions during the commercials and after the program.

After the show, express your ideas and opinions about it in small groups by answering these questions.

1. What happened during the show? (What were the events? What was the topic of discussion? etc.)

2. What was the point of the program or what points did it make? Do you agree or disagree with the ideas in it?

3. Did it meet your expectations? Why or why not? Would you watch the same show or another episode of it again? Why or why not?

*F. In watching T.V. at home, follow the steps in Exercise E. During the next class meeting, tell the class your ideas and opinions about what you have seen.

PART FOUR / EXPRESSING YOURSELF IN WRITING

● Short Essays

> Most essays, compositions, and papers are written as school assignments, but the organizational and writing skills taught in English classes can be useful in many other situations. Most essays follow a similar pattern:
>
> An introductory paragraph: a general indication of the purpose of the essay or a statement of the main points to be made
>
> The body of the essay: 3–8 paragraphs that develop the idea introduced in the first paragraph
>
> The concluding paragraph: a short, simple restatement or summary of the main idea

A.   *A First Draft*—To begin to write a short essay, you can follow these steps. Don't worry about grammar and other writing rules at first. Just put down your ideas as they come to mind. Leave space between lines so you can make corrections later.

1. Choose one of these topics about the media or make up one of your own.
   a. the effect of television on children
   b. the benefits or disadvantages of television (or radio or newspapers)
   c. the differences between television (or radio or newspapers) in this country and your own culture
   d. your favorite T.V. (or radio) program
   e. _____

2. On a piece of paper, write a general statement that indicates the purpose or introduces the main point of the essay you are going to write. **Example:**

   Television in my country serves the public interest better than T.V. in this country does.

3. Fill the rest of the piece of paper with ideas and phrases about what you are planning to write.

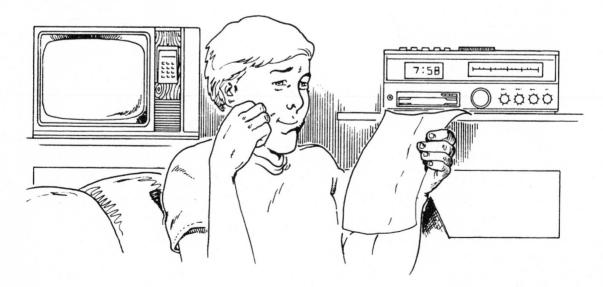

Outlining

Some writers make an outline before they begin to write. They may or may not follow the outline exactly in their essay, but it helps them to organize their thoughts. Here is one possible pattern for an outline of a paragraph in the body of an essay.

A topic sentence: a general statement about the topic of the paragraph

    1. A detail (a fact, opinion, reason, example, etc.) that supports the statement in the topic sentence

    2. Another detail

    3. Another detail

Sometimes writers also add "subdetails" to support the points of their paragraphs.

B. **Fill in the blanks of this outline with phrases from the essay that follows.**

A. The main idea of the essay: *The detrimental effects of the mass media outweigh its advantages*

B. Topic of Paragraph 2: _____

    1. Detail: _____

    2. Detail: _____

C. Topic of Paragraph 3: _____

    1. Detail: _____

    2. Detail: _____

    3. Detail: _____

    4. Detail: _____

D. Topic of Paragraph 4: _____

    1. Detail: _____

    2. Detail: _____

    3. Detail: _____

E. The concluding statement: _____

The Detrimental Effects of the Mass Media

Although there are a few ways in which viewers, listeners, and readers are benefited by the mass media, the detrimental effects of television, radio, magazines, and newspapers far outweigh the advantages.

Movie and T.V. scripts are carefully written to give us an unrealistic view of life. Most story characters are presented as either all good or all bad. People in real life are rarely so one-sided. In addition, happy endings are usually provided. The viewers learn to expect simple solutions to their problems and don't learn how to analyze issues and come up with realistic answers.

Another negative aspect of the media is the widespread use of unnecessary violence. Every night on T.V. dozens of violent incidents and murders can be seen, by young children as well as adults. Not only T.V. and radio news reports but also adventure and police shows are filled with people being injured or killed. Horribly violent movies, made to attract teenagers, bring in huge profits. Even popular songs can contain suggestions of violence.

Although advertising should be a source of information about new products, it has become a means of controlling our thoughts and values. Even if advertisements don't contain actual lies, they are likely to mislead viewers, listeners, or readers with their half-truths and omissions of facts. Many children are more interested in the quick, clever advertising they see on television than the educational shows made especially for them. Commercials have changed the values of this culture. The highest goals that the average person tries to achieve are materialistic ones.

Television, movies, radio, magazines, and newspapers—the mass media—could be used to inform, educate, and entertain. However, the media are being greatly misused and have many detrimental effects on our society.

_____ **C.** Use the phrases you wrote in Exercise A to make an outline for the essay you are going to write. (You can leave out unnecessary ideas and add better ones.) Your outline may not contain the same number of paragraphs, points, and subpoints as the above examples, but you should use the same kind of logic in its organization.

Connecting Words and Punctuation (Semicolons)

You can use connecting words and phrases to show the relationship between ideas in separate sentences. These connecting expressions are common at the beginning of a sentence, followed by a comma.

Addition	**Restatement**	**Contrast**
in addition	in other words	however
furthermore	i.e. (that is)	on the other hand

Result	**Examples**
therefore	for example
as a result	for instance

Two short, closely related sentences can be separated by a semicolon (;) rather than a period. A semicolon is often used before the connecting words and phrases in the above lists.

Examples:

The people must be kept informed; **furthermore**, they should be able to express their views.

Advertising gets many viewers to buy products they don't need; **on the other hand**, commercials can be amusing.

D.   Use the outline you wrote in Exercise C to write a short essay of your own, in four to ten paragraphs. Use connecting words and phrases to show the relationship between ideas. Then correct your grammar, punctuation, and spelling.

Exchange papers with a classmate and discuss the ideas in your essays. Ask and answer questions. Are there any points that you'd now like to omit, add, or change? You may want to rewrite your essay.

*E.   Summarize the point of view of your paper in a few sentences for the class. Then give it to a classmate who would like to write a short essay that expresses the opposite point of view. He or she writes a contrasting essay.

In small groups, read the two essays aloud. Decide which essay is stronger and summarize your discussion for the class.

CHAPTER

10

A Lifetime of Learning

READING AND WRITING FOCUS:
Attempts to persuade
Rules and regulations
Problem solving

NEW READING AND VOCABULARY SKILLS:
Distinguishing attempts to persuade from facts
Distinguishing objective from subjective language

WRITING SKILLS:
Using adjective, noun, and adverb clauses

GRAMMAR FOCUS:
Noun, adjective, and adverb clauses

PART ONE /READING FOR MEANING

● Reading Between the Lines

Previewing the Reading

A. **Prepare to read by making up a story about this picture. Answer these questions.**

1. What does the letter that the people are holding probably say?
2. What do you think these people are talking about and thinking?

B.   **Read the following selection quickly for important ideas.**

Many of the tenants of 1747 Esperanza Lane called one another up as soon as they'd read the letter that arrived today. This is what it said:

Greenback Investment and Development Corporation
1000 Bill Boulevard
Los Angeles, California 90051
(213) 555-5000

September 30, 19XX

Dear Tenant:

As the owners of the apartment complex at 1747 Esperanza Lane, we have been faced with a serious problem. Our efforts to provide high-quality property management have resulted in considerable financial losses. Unable to keep rising maintenance costs and other expenses to a minimum, we have been forced to choose from the following alternatives: raising rents substantially, putting the property up for sale to an individual buyer, or converting the complex into condominiums. We are pleased to announce that our corporation has decided on the third option.

As soon as it is available, you will be sent a prospectus (a proposed plan) that explains the condominium conversion in detail. The purpose of this letter is to inform you, our favored tenants, what the conversion process can mean to you.

Soon after our prospectus is approved, each of you will be offered the first opportunity to purchase the apartment unit in which you are now living. You can rest assured that our asking price will be far below what you would expect to pay for comparable condominiums in the immediate area. It is an "insider price," available only to present residents of the complex.

Those of you who have never owned your own home may be asking how condominium ownership will benefit you. First of all, there are financial advantages: if you consider the tax benefits of purchasing your unit, most of you will eventually end up paying less for your mortgage loan than you would be spending for monthly rent. Furthermore, when you own the apartment where you live, no landlord or owner can ever raise your rent. The main financial advantage, however, is that your property will be increasing in value from the day you take title to it; instead of losing that part of your income you have been paying for rent, you will be investing it in the future of your family.

If you could improve your apartment complex in any way that would make your living environment more comfortable and attractive, what would you do? Would you build a swimming pool or a recreation room? Provide a play area for young children? Hire a security guard for the parking area? As a member of your condominium association, you will have an important voice in the matters that affect your building and your lives.

We at the Greenback Investment and Development Corporation are proud to be able to make you this exciting offer. To those of you who decide to take advantage of this once-in-a-lifetime opportunity, we extend our congratulations in advance.

Respectfully yours,

I. Will Steele

I. Will Steele
Vice President
Real Estate Division

"I'm not sure what that all means," confided Giovanna Bevilacqua after she'd gone over the letter on the phone with Paulina Becerra. "But I know I don't like the sound of it."

"I'm not sure I follow you," responded her neighbor. "Everything the letter says is positive. I get the feeling that it's saying we'll be sorry if we don't jump at this chance."

"That's exactly my point!" exclaimed Giovanna. "All that the letter talks about are the so-called advantages of this condominium conversion. It doesn't tell us how much of a down payment will be required, how we can finance it,..."

"Or what condition the building is in, who will be fixing it up and providing maintenance, and so on," continued Paulina. "I suppose you're right. To find out what's important, I guess we'll have to read between the lines."

"But we're not alone in this," Giovanna reminded her. "I think we'd better call a meeting of all the tenants, do some research to get some objective information, hire an attorney to represent us in the negotiations, and deal with this situation as soon as possible."

_____ **C.** *Getting the Main Ideas*—Circle the letter of the correct words for each blank.

1. The tenants of 1747 Esperanza Lane were concerned about a letter announcing that _____.
   a. their building would be converted to condominiums
   b. their rents would be raised by 25 percent
   c. the complex was being sold to a savings and loan association

2. The owners of the building were claiming that they were forced to choose the option they did because _____.
   a. the real estate laws had been changed
   b. they had financial losses because of rising expenses
   c. they were too concerned abuot the tenants to consider raising rents

3. The letter they sent to the residents described _____.
   a. the financial liabilities of property ownership
   b. only the advantages of buying your own apartment
   c. the benefits and the disadvantages of condominium conversion

4. After the neighbors had read and discussed the letter, they decided to _____.
   a. apply for bank loans to be able to make the down payment
   b. have a tenants' meeting, get objective information, and hire a lawyer
   c. fight against the condominium conversion in a court of law

_____ **D.** *Distinguishing Attempts to Persuade from Facts*—Write *O* (objective) on the lines before the actual facts and *S* (subjective) before the statements used in attempts to persuade.

1. _S_ Our unsuccessful efforts at providing high-quality property management at low cost have forced us to convert to condominiums.

2. _____ Soon after the prospectus is approved, all apartment units will be offered for sale to the tenants living in them.

3. _____ Our asking price is a marvelous buy, far below the actual value of the property.

4. _____ Because your property will rise considerably in value, you will be making an excellent investment in the future.

5. _____ Your monthly mortgage payment will be 10 percent below what you are presently paying in rent.

6. _____ The tenants of the complex will form a condominium association to discuss matters of common concern.

_____ **E.**   **Now that you have read the story and the letter, look back at the picture on page 125 and answer the questions again.**

_____ **F.**   *Expressing Your Ideas*—Check each of the following statements that you agree with. In small groups, discuss the reasons for your answers. Then summarize your discussion for the class.

1. _____ A condominium conversion is an excellent opportunity for residents to become property owners and to make an investment.

2. _____ It is better to rent an apartment than to buy it because of the responsibility and expenses involved in ownership.

3. _____ Most language used in discussions of real estate deals is subjective rather than objective, and property developers shouldn't be trusted.

4. _____ Tenants should join together to make sure landlords don't take advantage of them.

PART TWO / VOCABULARY BUILDING

● Objective vs. Subjective Language

> Some words are more likely to appear in objective information, whereas others are more common in subjective statements that are attempts to persuade. Statements designed to appeal to the emotions should be examined critically; they may or may not be based on facts.

A. Considering the meanings of the underlined words, mark each of the sentences in the following pairs as positive (+) or negative (−).

1. _−_ You are <u>faced</u> with making a <u>serious</u> financial <u>decision</u>.

   _+_ You have been <u>offered</u> a <u>promising</u> financial <u>option</u>.

2. ___ The corporation has <u>exceeded</u> its budget through <u>mismanagement</u>.

   ___ The corporation has <u>spared no expense</u> in fulfilling its <u>responsibilities</u>.

3. ___ We are <u>pleased</u> to <u>announce</u> that you have the <u>opportunity</u> to become a property owner.

   ___ We are <u>sorry</u> to inform you that you <u>have no choice but</u> to finance the property.

B. Number the sentences in each group 1, 2, or 3. Put 1 on the line before the most subjective statement, 2 before the next most subjective one, and 3 before the most objective description of fact.

1. ___ With tax deductions, the amount you will be paying for your mortgage loan could be up to 10 percent less than your present rent payment.

   _1_ Our selling price is a marvelous, once-in-a-lifetime opportunity that you would be foolish to pass up.

   ___ You'll be paying considerably less for your own property than you're now giving your landlord for rent.

2. ___ It's likely that your property will be increasing in value from the day you take title to it.

   ___ The average condominium in your area has risen in value by about 30 percent in the last five years.

   ___ By investing in your own unit, you will be providing your loved ones with the future security they deserve.

3. ___ As a member of your condominium association, you will have a vote in the matters that affect your building.

   ___ By belonging to the condominium association, you will have the power to determine the future of your living environment.

   ___ You are required, as a condominium owner, to share responsibility for the common concerns of your association.

4. _____ The owners of your apartment complex will make every effort to reach an agreement that is fair and reasonable.

_____ Because the owners of your building are aware that the terms of a real estate deal are open to negotiation, they are willing to be present at a meeting of tenants.

_____ If you don't jump at the chance to accept the generous offer of the building owners, you will regret your decision later.

_____ ***C.** **To learn vocabulary, choose ten words from the reading selection "Reading Between the Lines" or something else you are reading that have either positive or negative associations. List as many synonyms for each word as you can. After marking each positive word with a + sign and each negative word with a – sign, make up sentences for two of the words in each list that illustrate the meaning.**

PART THREE / SCANNING FOR INFORMATION

● Rules and Regulations

> Like the language of contracts, the language in the documents of legal associations is usually much more formal and precise than that of everyday speech and writing. It is likely to consist of a long list of rules and regulations.

A. Scan these excerpts from a list of regulations for the owners and tenants in a condominium complex. Then answer these questions: Would you like to live in a complex with these rules? Why or why not?

A. No conduct is permitted on the premises that will increase the rate of insurance, cause the Association's current insurance policies to be canceled, or result in the uninsurability of the entire project.

B. No unit shall be used for any purpose other than single-family residential purposes. No gainful occupation, trade, or other nonresidential use shall be conducted on the premises, with the exception of professional and administrative occupations without any visible external evidence, so long as such occupations are in accordance with all applicable governmental ordinances and are merely incidental to the use of the unit as a residence.

C. Only one domestic animal, weighing under 25 pounds, is permitted per unit.

All pets, when outside the unit, must be kept on a leash.

Pet owners are responsible for immediate clean-up of their animal's waste.

D. All vehicles parked outside of assigned parking spaces or in the visitor parking spaces without temporary visitors' parking passes will be subject to towing without prior notice at the owner's/operator's sole expense.

E. No resident shall disturb any other resident's use or enjoyment of their unit by the use of noisy instruments such as wind chimes, bells, etc. The volume of televisions, stereos, radios, etc. should be turned down before 9:00 a.m. and after 10:00 p.m. No noises from within units that interfere with the rights, comforts, or conveniences of other residents, such as drums, other musical instruments, or loud parties, will be permitted at any time.

F. In the event of a plumbing malfunction, the Association will make the necessary repairs. If it is determined that the problem has been caused by improper use of the plumbing by a resident of a particular unit, or if it is determined that the malfunction was not a Common Area problem, the cost of such repair will be charged to the Homeowner responsible for the damage.

G. Laundry equipment is to be cleaned by the user after each use. Washing machines and dryers should be left free of any visible lint, dirt, or debris. No trash or garbage is to be left in laundry rooms except in the containers provided. Laundry room hours are from 8:00 a.m. to 11:00 p.m. daily.

H. All refuse shall be deposited with care in the trash chutes provided. Foodstuff should be wrapped in plastic bags. Under no circumstances is any garbage to be left in the corridor or trash rooms. Boxes and items too large for the trash chutes shall be deposited in the trash rooms on the ground floor. Keys to locked areas can be obtained from the business office.

B. Match these subjects with the rules excerpts in Exercise A by writing the letters *A–H* on the lines.

1. _D_ parking

2. ____ the use of the units

3. ____ the laundry rooms

4. ____ trash

5. ____ noise

6. ____ behavior and insurance

7. ____ pets

8. ____ plumbing

_____ **C.** Does the simplified sentence (b) in each pair have approximately the same meaning as the statement (a)? Write *yes* or *no* on the line.

1. _No_
   a. No conduct is permitted on the premises that will increase the rate of insurance.
   b. No one will be allowed to conduct an insurance business in his or her apartment unit.

2. _____
   a. No gainful occupation, trade, or other nonresidential use shall be conducted on the premises, with the exception of professional and administrative occupations without any visible external evidence.
   b. You can't run a business out of your home if there are signs, customers, etc., but you can bring work home from the office.

3. _____
   a. Only one domestic animal weighing under 25 pounds is permitted per unit.
   b. The owners or tenants of each apartment can have one pet, but it must be small.

4. _____
   a. All vehicles parked outside of assigned parking spaces or parked in the visitor parking spaces without temporary visitors' parking passes will be subject to towing without prior notice at the owner's/operator's sole expense.
   b. Because cars and trucks are the subject of considerable concern by visitors, parking assignments and passes will all be temporary.

5. _____
   a. No noises from within units that interfere with the rights, comforts, or conveniences of other residents will be permitted at any time.
   b. Owners and tenants can never play music or have parties.

6. _____
   a. All refuse shall be deposited with care in the trash chutes provided.
   b. Residents are responsible for throwing away their trash properly.

7. _____
   a. If it is determined that a plumbing problem has been caused by improper use of the plumbing by a resident of a particular unit, the cost of such repair will be charged to the homeowner responsible for the damage.
   b. If someone damages the plumbing, he or she has to pay for the repairs.

8. _____
   a. Washing machines and dryers should be left free of any visible lint, dirt, or debris.
   b. Apartment owners can use the laundry room free of charge if they don't leave dirt in the facilities.

_____ **D.** For the items in Exercise C that you answered *no* to, restate the meaning of sentence a.

_____ ***E.** Beyond the text: From an apartment manager, a housing office, or the library, bring to class a housing agreeement, a lease, or a list of rules and regulations. Make a list of questions that you, as a tenant or condominium owner, might ask before you moved into a new place.

EXAMPLES: 1. Can we keep pets?
   2. Are there any regulations about playing music?
   3. Is there a monthly fee for maintenance?

In turn, each student asks one of his or her questions, and all the other students find the answers in their documents as quickly as they can. After the sentence or sentences that give the relevant information are read aloud, the class "translates" the statements into more common, simpler language, if necessary.

PART FOUR /EXPRESSING YOURSELF IN WRITING

● Solving Problems

> When you need to solve a problem, it may help to put your thoughts and ideas
> in writing. Then you can define the situation accurately, suggest and evaluate
> possible solutions, and perhaps come to a conclusion.

A.

A First Draft—To begin the process of problem solving, you can work in a small group and follow these steps. Don't worry about grammar and other writing rules at first. Just put down your ideas as they come to mind. Leave space between lines so you can make corrections later.

1. As a group, decide on one sentence or phrase to describe the problem or situation.
   Example: conversion of an old apartment building into condominiums

2. As a group, decide on the points of most concern and then, individually, write a description of the situation. After all the papers are read aloud, the group will choose the best (the clearest and most complete) description of the problem. **Example:**

   > Since we received a letter telling us that that our building is going to be
   > converted into condominiums, we have been trying to figure out what to do.
   > After doing some market research, we have come to the conclusion that the
   > owner's asking price is about 10 percent below that of other condos in the
   > area; on the other hand, the building is older, and we have no information on
   > the condition of the roof, the wiring, etc., or on the repairs that might be
   > needed. Until we receive an accurate account of the ongoing expenses on the
   > building (taxes, maintenance, etc.), we will not be able to estimate the cost of
   > condo conversion to each tenant. Furthermore, it is unlikely that all of the
   > present residents could either come up with the requested down payment or
   > qualify for a bank loan.

3. Individually, decide on the best solution to the problem and write it as the second paragraph of your paper. In turn, read your solution aloud to the group, which will decide on the best (the most workable and reasonable) solution. **Example:**

   > Since all property deals are open to negotiation, I suggest calling a
   > tenants' meeting to discuss the owner's offer. As soon as we have agreed on a
   > course of action, we can invite the owner or his representatives to meet with
   > us. Some of the issues we should be discussing are: lowering the selling price
   > of each unit to current residents, working out financing with the owner,
   > requiring the owner to make necessary repairs before selling the units, and so
   > on. Of course, we should also hire an attorney to represent us in these
   > negotiations.

4. Summarize the group's chosen problem and the solution that you agreed on for the class.

> Most formal writing consists of full sentences, each of which contains at least one subject and one verb phrase. Adjective, noun, or adverb clauses (not independent sentences) can be added.
>
> **Examples:**
>
> The building **that you live in** (*an adjective clause*) has been sold to a new owner **who wishes to tear it down** (*an adjective clause*).
>
> The development corporation is pleased to announce **that it will be building a modern apartment complex on the site** (*a noun clause*).
>
> **As soon as it is available** (*an introductory adverb clause followed by a comma*), you will be sent a prospectus **that explains the terms of our plan** (*an adjective clause*).
>
> We don't know **what we should do** (*a noun clause*) because housing is very **expensive in our city** (*an adverb clause*).
>
> The news was so unexpected **that the tenants don't know where to look for new housing** (*a noun clause within an adverb clause*).

B.   **Join the two sentences in each pair, by making one of them into an adverb clause, and using the connecting words in parentheses. Then write all of your new sentences in paragraph form.**

1. Our apartment building is being sold. It has not been bringing in much income to the present owner. (because)

   Our apartment building is being sold because it has not been bringing in much income to the present owner.

2. The building is in bad condition. The new owners will probably not want to fix it up. (such...that)

3. They may want to tear it down right away. They don't lose money on it. (so that)

4. However, the property doesn't meet the requirements for commercial development. The city may not give the owners a building permit. (if)

5. Perhaps they'll choose to completely renovate the building and raise the rents. Most of the tenants can't afford to pay more for housing. (even though)

6. They may decide to convert the building to condominiums. It's been renovated and modernized. (after)

_____ **C.** Correct the errors in the underlined adjective, noun, and adverb clauses. (Remember that these clauses cannot appear as independent sentences and should not be run into other sentences without connecting words.)

The idea of condominium conversion may be attractive to apartment owners ~~aren't~~ *who* aren't
∧1.

making much money from the rents they're collecting ~~them~~. In addition, there may be
2.

tax advantages to the conversion process <u>what the owners wouldn't receive</u> <u>if were sold</u>
3.   4.

the buildings as is. However, the conversion process isn't <u>easy so that the owners can</u>
5.

simply put the units up for sale. There are rules for condominium conversions. <u>Even</u>
6.

<u>though they vary from state to state.</u> Owners can't simply give tenants notice, for

instance. <u>That they have to move by a certain time.</u> Some states have laws <u>require them</u>
7.   8.

<u>to get at least 50 percent of the present residents to sign a "notice of intention to</u>

<u>purchase"</u> their application is approved before. <u>Some residents may want to move others</u>
9.   10.

may want or need to stay <u>just where are they</u> and wouldn't know <u>how or where they</u>
11.   12.

<u>could find a comfortable place to live in the same price range.</u>

_____ **D.** Revise the draft you wrote in Exercise A about a problem and a possible solution, using adjective, noun, and adverb clauses when possible and natural. Then correct your grammar, punctuation, and spelling.

_____ ***E.** Exchange papers with a classmate who has written about another problem. Is the explanation of the problem you have received clear? If not, ask the writer questions about it. Do you agree with the suggested solution? If not, write a solution of your own, give it to your partner, and discuss the advantages of your ideas.